RESUMES
FOR
MIDCAREER
JOB CHANGES

Professional Resumes Series

RESUMES
FOR
MIDCAREER
JOB CHANGES

The Editors of
VGM Career Horizons

Printed on recyclable paper

 **VGM Career Horizons**
a division of *NTC Publishing Group*
Lincolnwood, Illinois USA

ACKNOWLEDGMENT

The editors gratefully acknowledge Jeffrey S. Johnson and Cheryl R. McLean for their help in the writing and production of this book.

Library of Congress Cataloging-in-Publication Data

Resumes for midcareer job changes
     p.   cm.—(VGM professional resumes series)

ISBN 0-8442-4155-5
   1. Résumés (Employment) 2. Career changes. I. Title.
II. Series: VGM's professional resumes series.
HF5383.M34 1993
808′.066651—dc20   92-47435
                                      CIP

1996 Printing

Published by VGM Career Horizons, a division of NTC Publishing Group.
© 1993 by NTC Publishing Group, 4255 West Touhy Avenue,
Lincolnwood (Chicago), Illinois 60646-1975 U.S.A.
Manufactured in the United States of America.

6 7 8 9 0 VP 9 8 7 6 5 4 3

CONTENTS

Introduction   vii

Chapter One
The Elements of a Good Resume   1

Chapter Two
Writing Your Resume   15

Chapter Three
Assembly and Layout   19

Chapter Four
The Cover Letter   27

Chapter Five
Sample Resumes   29

Chapter Six
Sample Cover Letters   131

Introduction

Your resume is your first impression on a prospective employer. Though you may be articulate, intelligent, and charming in person, a poor resume may prevent you from ever having the opportunity to demonstrate your interpersonal skills, because a poor resume may prevent you from ever being called for an interview. While few people have ever been hired solely on the basis of their resume, a well-written, well-organized resume can go a long way toward helping you land an interview. Your resume's main purpose is to get you that interview. The rest is up to you and the employer. If you both feel that you are right for the job and the job is right for you, chances are you will be hired.

A resume must catch the reader's attention yet still be easy to read and to the point. Resume styles have changed over the years. Today, brief and focused resumes are preferred. No longer do employers have the patience, or the time, to review several pages of solid type. A resume should be only one page long, if possible, and never more than two pages. Time is a precious commodity in today's business world and the resume that is concise and straightforward will usually be the one that gets noticed.

Let's not make the mistake, though, of assuming that writing a brief resume means that you can take less care in preparing it. A successful resume takes time and thought, and if you are willing to make the effort, the rewards are well worth it. Think of your resume as a sales tool with the product being you. You want to sell yourself to a prospective employer. This book is designed to help you prepare a resume that will help you further your career—to land that next job, or first job, or to return to the work force after years of absence. So, read on. Make the effort and reap the rewards that a strong resume can bring to your career. Let's get to it!

Chapter One

THE ELEMENTS OF A GOOD RESUME

A winning resume is made of the elements that employers are most interested in seeing when reviewing a job applicant. These basic elements are the essential ingredients of a successful resume and become the actual sections of your resume. The following is a list of elements that may be used in a resume. Some are essential; some are optional. We will be discussing these in this chapter in order to give you a better understanding of each element's role in the makeup of your resume:

1. Heading
2. Objective
3. Work Experience
4. Education
5. Honors
6. Activities
7. Certificates and Licenses
8. Professional Memberships
9. Special Skills
10. Personal Information
11. References

The first step in preparing your resume is to gather together information about yourself and your past accomplishments. Later you will refine this information, rewrite it in the most effective language, and organize it into the most attractive layout. First, let's take a look at each of these important elements individually.

Heading

The heading may seem to be a simple enough element in your resume, but be careful not to take it lightly. The heading should be placed at the top of your resume and should include your name, home address, and telephone numbers. If you can take calls at your current place of business, include your business number, since most employers will attempt to contact you during the business day. If this is not possible, or if you can afford it, purchase an answering machine that allows you to retrieve your messages while you are away from home. This way you can make sure you don't miss important phone calls. *Always* include your phone number on your resume. It is crucial that when prospective employers need to have immediate contact with you, they can.

Objective

When seeking a particular career path, it is important to list a job objective on your resume. This statement helps employers know the direction that you see yourself heading, so that they can determine whether your goals are in line with the position available. The objective is normally one sentence long and describes your employment goals clearly and concisely. See the sample resumes in this book for examples of objective statements.

The job objective will vary depending on the type of person you are, the field you are in, and the type of goals you have. It can be either specific or general, but it should always be to the point.

In some cases, this element is not necessary, but usually it is a good idea to include your objective. It gives your possible future employer an idea of where you are coming from and where you want to go.

The objective statement is better left out, however, if you are uncertain of the exact title of the job you seek. In such a case, the inclusion of an overly specific objective statement could result in your not being considered for a variety of acceptable positions; you should be sure to incorporate this information in your cover letter, instead.

Work Experience

This element is arguably the most important of them all. It will provide the central focus of your resume, so it is necessary that this section be as complete as possible. Only by examining your work experience in depth can you get to the heart of your accomplishments and present them in a way that demonstrates the strength of your qualifications. Of course, someone just out of school will have less work experience than someone who has been working for a number of years, but the amount of information isn't the most important thing—rather, how it is presented and how it highlights you as a person and as a worker will be what counts.

As you work on this section of your resume, be aware of the need for accuracy. You'll want to include all necessary information about each of your jobs, including job title, dates, employer, city, state, responsibilities, special projects, and accomplishments. Be sure to only list company accomplishments for which you were directly responsible. If you haven't participated in any special projects, that's all right—this area may not be relevant to certain jobs.

The most common way to list your work experience is in *reverse chronological order*. In other words, start with your most recent job and work your way backwards. This way your prospective employer sees your current (and often most important) job before seeing your past jobs. Your most recent position, if the most important, should also be the one that includes the most information, as compared to your previous positions. If you are just out of school, show your summer employment and part-time work, though in this case your education will most likely be more important than your work experience.

The following worksheets will help you gather information about your past jobs.

WORK EXPERIENCE
Job One:

Job Title _____

Dates _____

Employer _____

City, State _____

Major Duties _____

_____

_____

_____

_____

_____

_____

_____

Special Projects _____

_____

_____

_____

Accomplishments _____

_____

_____

_____

_____

_____

_____

_____

Job Two:

Job Title _____

Dates _____

Employer _____

City, State _____

Major Duties _____

_____

_____

_____

_____

_____

_____

_____

Special Projects _____

_____

_____

_____

Accomplishments _____

_____

_____

_____

_____

_____

_____

_____

_____

Job Three:

Job Title _____

Dates _____

Employer _____

City, State _____

Major Duties _____

_____

_____

_____

_____

_____

_____

Special Projects _____

_____

_____

_____

Accomplishments _____

_____

_____

_____

_____

_____

_____

_____

_____

Job Four:

Job Title _____

Dates _____

Employer _____

City, State _____

Major Duties _____

_____

_____

_____

_____

_____

_____

_____

_____

Special Projects _____

_____

_____

_____

Accomplishments _____

_____

_____

_____

_____

_____

_____

_____

_____

Education

Education is the second most important element of a resume. Your educational background is often a deciding factor in an employer's decision to hire you. Be sure to stress your accomplishments in school with the same finesse that you stressed your accomplishments at work. If you are looking for your first job, your education will be your greatest asset, since your work experience will most likely be minimal. In this case, the education section becomes the most important. You will want to be sure to include any degrees or certificates you received, your major area of concentration, any honors, and any relevant activities. Again, be sure to list your most recent schooling first. If you have completed graduate-level work, begin with that and work in reverse chronological order through your undergraduate education. If you have completed an undergraduate degree, you may choose whether to list your high school experience or not. This should be done only if your high school grade-point average was well above average.

The following worksheets will help you gather information for this section of your resume. Also included are supplemental worksheets for honors and for activities. Sometimes honors and activities are listed in a section separate from education, most often near the end of the resume.

EDUCATION

School _____

Major or Area of Concentration _____

Degree _____

Date _____

School _____

Major or Area of Concentration _____

Degree _____

Date _____

Honors

Here, you should list any awards, honors, or memberships in honorary societies that you have received. Usually these are of an academic nature, but they can also be for special achievement in sports, clubs, or other school activities. Always be sure to include the name of the organization honoring you and the date(s) received. Use the worksheet below to help gather your honors information.

HONORS

Honor: _____

Awarding Organization: _____

Date(s): _____

Honor: _____

Awarding Organization: _____

Date(s): _____

Honor: _____

Awarding Organization: _____

Date(s): _____

Honor: _____

Awarding Organization: _____

Date(s): _____

Activities

You may have been active in different organizations or clubs during your years at school; often an employer will look at such involvement as evidence of initiative and dedication. Your ability to take an active role, and even a leadership role, in a group should be included on your resume. Use the worksheet provided to list your activities and accomplishments in this area. In general, you should exclude any organization the name of which indicates the race, creed, sex, age, marital status, color, or nation of origin of its members.

ACTIVITIES

Organization/Activity: _____

Accomplishments: _____

_____

_____

Organization/Activity: _____

Accomplishments: _____

_____

_____

Organization/Activity: _____

Accomplishments: _____

_____

_____

Organization/Activity: _____

Accomplishments: _____

_____

_____

As your work experience increases through the years, your school activities and honors will play less of a role in your resume, and eventually you will most likely only list your degree and any major honors you received. This is due to the fact that, as time goes by, your job performance becomes the most important element in your resume. Through time, your resume should change to reflect this.

Certificates and Licenses

The next potential element of your resume is certificates and licenses. You should list these if the job you are seeking requires them and you, of course, have acquired them. If you have applied for a license, but have not yet received it, use the phrase "application pending."

License requirements vary by state. If you have moved or you are planning to move to another state, be sure to check with the appropriate board or licensing agency in the state in which you are applying for work to be sure that you are aware of all licensing requirements.

Always be sure that all of the information you list is completely accurate. Locate copies of your licenses and certificates and check the exact date and name of the accrediting agency. Use the following worksheet to list your licenses and certificates.

CERTIFICATES AND LICENSES

Name of License: _____

Licensing Agency: _____

Date Issued: _____

Name of License: _____

Licensing Agency: _____

Date Issued: _____

Name of License: _____

Licensing Agency: _____

Date Issued: _____

Professional Memberships

Another potential element in your resume is a section listing professional memberships. Use this section to list involvement in professional associations, unions, and similar organizations. It is to your advantage to list any professional memberships that pertain to the job you are seeking. Be sure to include the dates of your involvement and whether you took part in any special activities or held any offices within the organization. Use the following worksheet to gather your information.

PROFESSIONAL MEMBERSHIPS

Name of Organization: _____

Offices Held: _____

Activities: _____

Date(s): _____

Name of Organization: _____

Offices Held: _____

Activities: _____

Date(s): _____

Name of Organization: _____

Offices Held: _____

Activities: _____

Date(s): _____

Name of Organization: _____

Offices Held: _____

Activities: _____

Date(s): _____

Special Skills

This section of your resume is set aside for mentioning any special abilities you have that could relate to the job you are seeking. This is the part of your resume where you have the opportunity to demonstrate certain talents and experiences that are not necessarily a part of your educational or work experience. Common examples include fluency in a foreign language, or knowledge of a particular computer application.

Special skills can encompass a wide range of your talents—remember to be sure that whatever skills you list relate to the type of work you are looking for.

Personal Information

Some people include "Personal" information on their resumes. This is not generally recommended, but you might wish to include it if you think that something in your personal life, such as a hobby or talent, has some bearing on the position you are seeking. This type of information is often referred to at the beginning of an interview, when it is used as an "ice breaker." Of course, personal information regarding age, marital status, race, religion, or sexual preference should never appear on any resume.

References

References are not usually listed on the resume, but a prospective employer needs to know that you have references who may be contacted if necessary. All that is necessary to include in your resume regarding references is a sentence at the bottom stating, "References are available upon request." If a prospective employer requests a list of references, be sure to have one ready. Also, check with whomever you list to see if it is all right for you to use them as a reference. Forewarn them that they may receive a call regarding a reference for you. This way they can be prepared to give you the best reference possible.

Chapter Two

WRITING YOUR RESUME

Now that you have gathered together all of the information for each of the sections of your resume, it's time to write out each section in a way that will get the attention of whoever is reviewing it. The type of language you use in your resume will affect its success. You want to take the information you have gathered and translate it into a language that will cause a potential employer to sit up and take notice.

Resume writing is not like expository writing or creative writing. It embodies a functional, direct writing style and focuses on the use of action words. By using action words in your writing, you more effectively stress past accomplishments. Action words help demonstrate your initiative and highlight your talents. Always use verbs that show strength and reflect the qualities of a "doer." By using action words, you characterize yourself as a person who takes action, and this will impress potential employers.

The following is a list of verbs commonly used in resume writing. Use this list to choose the action words that can help your resume become a strong one:

administered

advised

analyzed

arranged

assembled

assumed responsibility

billed

built

carried out

channeled

collected

communicated

compiled

completed

conducted

contacted

contracted

coordinated

counseled

created

cut

designed

determined

developed

directed

dispatched

distributed

documented

edited

established

expanded

functioned as

gathered

handled

hired

implemented

improved

inspected

interviewed

introduced

invented

maintained

managed

met with

motivated

negotiated

operated

orchestrated

ordered

organized

oversaw

performed

planned

prepared

presented

produced

programmed

published

purchased

recommended

recorded

reduced

referred

represented

researched

reviewed

saved

screened

served as

served on

sold

suggested

supervised

taught

tested

trained

typed

wrote

Now take a look at the information you put down on the work experience worksheets. Take that information and rewrite it in paragraph form, using verbs to highlight your actions and accomplishments. Let's look at an example, remembering that what matters here is the writing style, and not the particular job responsibilities given in our sample.

WORK EXPERIENCE
Regional Sales Manager

Manager of sales representatives from seven states. Responsible for twelve food chain accounts in the East. In charge of directing the sales force in planned selling toward specific goals. Supervisor and trainer of new sales representatives. Consulting for customers in the areas of inventory management and quality control.

Special Projects: Coordinator and sponsor of annual food industry sales seminar.

Accomplishments: Monthly regional volume went up 25 percent during my tenure while, at the same time, a proper sales/cost ratio was maintained. Customer/company relations improved significantly.

Below is the rewritten version of this information, using action words. Notice how much stronger it sounds.

WORK EXPERIENCE
Regional Sales Manager

Managed sales representatives from seven states. Handled twelve food chain accounts in the eastern United States. Directed the sales force in planned selling towards specific goals. Supervised and trained new sales representatives. Consulted for customers in the areas of inventory management and quality control. Coordinated and sponsored the annual Food Industry Seminar. Increased monthly regional volume 25 percent and helped to improve customer/company relations during my tenure.

Another way of constructing the work experience section is by using actual job descriptions. Job descriptions are rarely written using the proper resume language, but they do include all the information necessary to create this section of your resume. Take the description of one of the jobs your are including on your resume (if you have access to it), and turn it into an action-oriented paragraph. Below is an example of a job description followed by a version of the same description written using action words. Again, pay attention to the style of writing, as the details of your own work experience will be unique.

PUBLIC ADMINISTRATOR I

Responsibilities: Coordinate and direct public services to meet the needs of the nation, state, or community. Analyze problems; work with special committees and public agencies; recommend solutions to governing bodies.

Aptitudes and Skills: Ability to relate to and communicate with people; solve complex problems through analysis; plan, organize, and implement policies and programs. Knowledge of political systems; financial management; personnel administration; program evaluation; organizational theory.

WORK EXPERIENCE
Public Administrator I

Wrote pamphlets and conducted discussion groups to inform citizens of legislative processes and consumer issues. Organized and supervised 25 interviewers. Trained interviewers in effective communication skills.

Now that you have learned how to word your resume, you are ready for the next step in your quest for a winning resume: assembly and layout.

Chapter Three

ASSEMBLY AND LAYOUT

*A*t this point, you've gathered all the necessary information for your resume, and you've rewritten it using the language necessary to impress potential employers. Your next step is to assemble these elements in a logical order and then to lay them out on the page neatly and attractively in order to achieve the desired effect: getting that interview.

Assembly

The order of the elements in a resume makes a difference in its overall effect. Obviously, you would not want to put your name and address in the middle of the resume or your special skills section at the top. You want to put the elements in an order that stresses your most important achievements, not the less pertinent information. For example, if you recently graduated from school and have no full-time work experience, you will want to list your education before you list any part-time jobs you may have held during school. On the other hand, if you have been gainfully employed for several years and currently hold an important position in your company, you will want to list your work experience ahead of your education, which has become less pertinent with time.

There are some elements that are always included in your resume and some that are optional. Following is a list of essential and optional elements:

Essential	*Optional*
Name	Job Objective
Address	Honors
Phone Number	Special Skills
Work Experience	Professional Memberships
Education	Activities
References Phrase	Certificates and Licenses
	Personal Information

Your choice of optional sections depends on your own background and employment needs. Always use information that will put you and your abilities in a favorable light. If your honors are impressive, then be sure to include them in your resume. If your activities in school demonstrate particular talents necessary for the job you are seeking, then allow space for a section on activities. Each resume is unique, just as each person is unique.

Types of Resumes

So far, our discussion about resumes has involved the most common type—the *reverse chronological* resume, in which your most recent job is listed first and so on. This is the type of resume usually preferred by human resources directors, and it is the one most frequently used. However, in some cases this style of presentation is not the most effective way to highlight your skills and accomplishments.

For someone reentering the work force after many years or someone looking to change career fields, the *functional resume* may work best. This type of resume focuses more on achievement and less on the sequence of your work history. In the functional resume, your experience is presented by what you have accomplished and the skills you have developed in your past work.

A functional resume can be assembled from the same information you collected for your chronological resume. The main difference lies in how you organize this information. Essentially, the work experience section becomes two sections, with your job duties and accomplishments comprising one section and your employer's name, city, state, your position, and the dates employed making up another section. The first section is placed near the top of the resume, just below the job objective section, and can be called *Accomplishments* or *Achievements*. The second section, containing the bare essentials of your employment history, should come after the accomplishments section and can be titled *Work Experience* or *Employment History*. The other sections of your resume remain the same. The work experience section is the only one affected in the functional resume. By placing the section that focuses on your achievements first, you thereby draw attention to these achievements. This puts less emphasis on who you worked for and more emphasis on what you did and what you are capable of doing.

For someone changing careers, emphasis on skills and achievements is essential. The identities of previous employers, which may be unrelated to one's new job field, need to be downplayed. The functional resume accomplishes this task. For someone reentering the work force after many years, a functional resume is the obvious choice. If you lack full-time work experience, you will need to draw attention away from this fact and instead focus on your skills and abilities gained possibly through volunteer activities or part-time work. Education may also play a more important role in this resume.

Which type of resume is right for you will depend on your own personal circumstances. It may be helpful to create a chronological *and* a functional resume and then compare the two to find out which is more suitable. The sample resumes found in this book include both chronological and functional resumes. Use these resumes as guides to help you decide on the content and appearance of your own resume.

Layout

Once you have decided which elements to include in your resume and you have arranged them in an order that makes sense and emphasizes your achievements and abilities, then it is time to work on the physical layout of your resume.

There is no single appropriate layout that applies to every resume, but there are a few basic rules to follow in putting your resume on paper:

1. Leave a comfortable margin on the sides, top, and bottom of the page (usually 1 to 1 1/2 inches).

2. Use appropriate spacing between the sections (usually 2 to 3 line spaces are adequate).

3. Be consistent in the *type* of headings you use for the different sections of your resume. For example, if you capitalize the heading EMPLOYMENT HISTORY, don't use initial capitals and underlining for a heading of equal importance, such as Education.

4. Always try to fit your resume onto one page. If you are having trouble fitting all your information onto one page, perhaps you are trying to say too much. Try to edit out any repetitive or unnecessary information or possibly shorten descriptions of earlier jobs. Be ruthless. Maybe you've included too many optional sections.

CHRONOLOGICAL RESUME

Franklin Wu
5391 Southward Plaza
Walnut Creek, CA 94596
(510) 555-9008

JOB OBJECTIVE: To obtain a position as a high-level optician in a fast-paced retail store.

EDUCATION: Graduated Hayward Community College, Hayward, CA in June of 1986.

Graduated North Central High School, Chicago, IL in June of 1984.

WORK EXPERIENCE:

1990 - present Great Spectacles, Walnut Creek, CA
Management Optician

1988 - 1990 Valley Vision, Pleasanton, CA
Management Optician and Frame Buyer

1986 - 1988 Dublin Optometry, Dublin, CA
File Clerk

SPECIAL QUALIFICATIONS: People person; fashion styling experience; knowledge of adjustments, repairs and fittings of glasses and contact lenses.

CERTIFICATION: American Board of Optometry Certificate

CLASSES AND SEMINARS: Cal-Q Optics to prepare for licensing, 1992
Opti-Fair - annual, three day seminars

REFERENCES: George Jones, O.D.
Great Spectacles, (510) 555-8941

Maria Lazar, Optician
Valley Vision, (510) 555-3726

FUNCTIONAL RESUME

RESUME OF QUALIFICATIONS
OF
PATRICIA WHITE

987 West 44th Street
Cheyenne, WY 82001
(307) 555-9872

PROFESSIONAL OBJECTIVE

Opportunity to demonstrate superior managerial ability and administrative decision-making skills in a nursing home environment.

SUMMARY OF QUALIFICATIONS

- Highly organized and motivated.

- Ability and patience to train and develop office and professional staff.

- Thorough knowledge of computers - IBM PC, Lotus 1-2-3, WordPerfect, Symphony Data Base, IBM 38, typing, 10-key by touch, dictaphone, and 2-way radio system.

- Extensive experience in all phases of geriatric care: management, accounting, and medical treatment.

- Good rapport with all levels of employees, patients and their families, and public agencies.

EDUCATION

University of Wyoming, B.A. Business
Laramie, WY

EXPERIENCE

1985-Present - Assistant Director, Longview Manor, Cheyenne, WY

1983-1985 - Business Manager, Mountain Top Nursing Home, Cheyenne, WY

REFERENCES

Excellent professional and personal references

Don't let the idea of having to tell every detail about your life get in the way of producing a resume that is simple and straightforward. The more compact your resume, the easier it will be to read and the better an impression it will make for you.

In some cases, the resume will not fit on a single page, even after extensive editing. In such cases, the resume should be printed on two pages so as not to compromise clarity or appearance. Each page of a two-page resume should be marked clearly with your name and the page number, e.g., "Judith Ramirez, page 1 of 2." The pages should then be stapled together.

Try experimenting with various layouts until you find one that looks good to you. Always show your final layout to other people and ask them what they like or dislike about it, and what impresses them most about your resume. Make sure that is what you want most to emphasize. If it isn't, you may want to consider making changes in your layout until the necessary information is emphasized. Use the sample resumes in this book to get some ideas for laying out your resume.

Putting Your Resume in Print

Your resume should be typed or printed on good quality $8^{1}/_{2}'' \times 11''$ bond paper. You want to make as good an impression as possible with your resume; therefore, quality paper is a necessity. If you have access to a word processor with a good printer, or know of someone who does, make use of it. Typewritten resumes should only be used when there are no other options available.

After you have produced a clean original, you will want to make duplicate copies of it. Usually a copy shop is your best bet for producing copies without smudges or streaks. Make sure you have the copy shop use quality bond paper for all copies of your resume. Ask for a sample copy before they run your entire order. After copies are made, check each copy for cleanliness and clarity.

Another more costly option is to have your resume typeset and printed by a printer. This will provide the most attractive resume of all. If you anticipate needing a lot of copies of your resume, the cost of having it typeset may be justified.

Proofreading

After you have finished typing the master copy of your resume and before you go to have it copied or printed, you must thoroughly check it for typing and spelling errors. Have several people read it over just in case you may have missed an error. Misspelled words and typing mistakes will not make a good impression on a prospective employer, as they are a bad reflection on your writing ability and your attention to detail. With thorough and conscientious proofreading, these mistakes can be avoided.

The following are some rules of capitalization and punctuation that may come in handy when proofreading your resume:

Rules of Capitalization

- Capitalize proper nouns, such as names of schools, colleges, and universities, names of companies, and brand names of products.
- Capitalize major words in the names and titles of books, tests, and articles that appear in the body of your resume.
- Capitalize words in major section headings of your resume.
- Do not capitalize words just because they seem important.
- When in doubt, consult a manual of style such as *Words Into Type* (Prentice-Hall), or *The Chicago Manual of Style* (The University of Chicago Press). Your local library can help you locate these and other reference books.

Rules of Punctuation

- Use a comma to separate words in a series.
- Use a semicolon to separate series of words that already include commas within the series.
- Use a semicolon to separate independent clauses that are not joined by a conjunction.
- Use a period to end a sentence.
- Use a colon to show that the examples or details that follow expand or amplify the preceding phrase.
- Avoid the use of dashes.
- Avoid the use of brackets.
- If you use any punctuation in an unusual way in your resume, be consistent in its use.
- Whenever you are uncertain, consult a style manual.

Chapter Four

THE COVER LETTER

*O*nce your resume has been assembled, laid out, and printed to your satisfaction, the next and final step before distribution is to write your cover letter. Though there may be instances where you deliver your resume in person, most often you will be sending it through the mail. Resumes sent through the mail always need an accompanying letter that briefly introduces you and your resume. The purpose of the cover letter is to get a potential employer to read your resume, just as the purpose of your resume is to get that same potential employer to call you for an interview.

Like your resume, your cover letter should be clean, neat, and direct. A cover letter usually includes the following information:

1. Your name and address.

2. The date.

3. The name and address of the person and company to whom you are sending your resume.

4. The salutation ("Dear Mr." or "Dear Ms." followed by the person's last name, or "To Whom It May Concern").

5. An opening paragraph explaining why you are writing (in response to an ad, the result of a previous meeting, at the suggestion of someone you both know) and indicating your interest in the job being offered.

6. One or two more paragraphs that tell why you want to work for the company and what qualifications and experience you can bring to that company.

7. A final paragraph that closes the letter and requests that you be contacted for an interview. You may mention here that your references are available upon request.

8. The closing ("Sincerely," or "Yours Truly," followed by your signature with your name typed under it).

Your cover letter, including all of the information above, should be no more than one page in length. The language used should be polite, businesslike, and to the point. Do not attempt to tell your life story in the cover letter. A long and cluttered letter will only serve to put off the reader. Remember, you only need to mention a few of your accomplishments and skills in the cover letter. The rest of your information is in your resume. Each and every achievement should not be mentioned twice. If your cover letter is a success, your resume will be read and all pertinent information reviewed by your prospective employer.

Producing the Cover Letter

Cover letters should always be typed individually, since they are always written to particular individuals and companies. Never use a form letter for your cover letter. Each one should be as personal as possible. Of course, once you have written and rewritten your first cover letter to the point where you are satisfied with it, you certainly can use similar wording in subsequent letters.

After you have typed your cover letter on quality bond paper, be sure to proofread it as thoroughly as you did your resume. Again, spelling errors are a sure sign of carelessness, and you don't want that to be a part of your first impression on a prospective employer. Make sure to handle the letter and resume carefully to avoid any smudges, and then mail both your cover letter and resume in an appropriate sized envelope. Be sure to keep an accurate record of all the resumes you send out and the results of each mailing.

Numerous sample cover letters appear at the end of the book. Use them as models for your own cover letter or to get an idea of how cover letters are put together. Remember, every one is unique and depends on the particular circumstances of the individual writing it and the job for which he or she is applying.

About a week after mailing resumes and cover letters to potential employers, you will want to contact them by telephone. Confirm that your resume arrived, and ask whether an interview might be possible. Getting your foot in the door during this call is half the battle of a job search, and a strong resume and cover letter will help you immeasurably.

Chapter Five

SAMPLE RESUMES

This chapter contains dozens of sample resumes for people pursuing a wide variety of jobs and careers. There are many different styles of resumes in terms of graphic layout and presentation of information. These samples also represent people with varying amounts of education and work experience. Use these samples to model your own resume after. Choose one resume, or borrow elements from several different resumes to help you construct your own.

SHARYL X. WILSON
84 Saratoga Avenue
Detroit, MI 48229
(313) 555-9388

SUMMARY: Sales and Marketing Manager with proven ability to conceptualize, structure, and achieve both market and profit objectives seeks to join the sales and marketing team of Chrysler Corporation.

ACHIEVEMENTS:

Sales

▼ Initiated sales incentive program to motivate the sales force to generate new product sales.

▼ Increased sales of recycled paper products from $250,000 to $600,000 in the first year. Successfully built sales to over $3,000,000 over the next five years.

▼ Held total responsibility for sales of copy-type papers, which represented 40 percent of total sales volume. Supervised six sales professionals.

▼ Initiated aggressive sales efforts for additional volume, allowing increased production using idle equipment, which spread costs and substantially improved profits.

▼ Strongly successful in developing new corporate accounts.

▼ Improved profitability by stressing quality and service and eliminating volume price contracts, which were depressing profits.

Management and Marketing

▼ Created and implemented the Neighborhood Business Strategy concentrating sales efforts to develop business close to the mill, effectively reducing costs and improving profitability.

▼ Changed company image from volume supplier to a dedicated quality product producer and provider of top-level customer service, a strategy that enhanced repeat business.

▼ Assumed newly created position, established its purpose, and made it work profitably. Established specifications, pricing, and developed marketing strategies.

▼ Implemented advertising campaigns with assistance from ad agencies.

▼ Supervised regional salesmen and helped their customers to develop greater product use and customer satisfaction.

EMPLOYMENT EXPERIENCE:

National Sales Manager, Starnes Paper, Subsidiary of Weyerhaeuser, Inc., Detroit, MI, 1984-present

Regional Sales Manager, James River, Inc., Grand Rapids, MI, 1975-1984

Regional Sales Manager, Specialty Papers, Greenfield Paper Company, Subsidiary of James River, Inc., Grand Rapids, MI, 1972-1975

Sales Manager, Greenfield Paper Company, Grand Rapids, MI, 1963-1972

EDUCATION:
M.B.A., Harvard University, Cambridge, MA, 1963
B.S., Business and Economics, University of California, Berkeley, 1961

REFERENCES AVAILABLE UPON REQUEST

Yoshio Umeki • 9783 Ridgeway Drive • Evanston, IL 60204 • 708 555-2983

Objective

A position as Publicist for a Midwest corporation or agency

Summary of Qualifications
- Skilled at working with the public
- Experienced and published writer
- Accustomed to working with deadlines
- Flexible and hardworking
- Knowledgeable about local government, business, and community

History of Employment

News Reporter, *Chicago Tribune,* 1985-present.
Specialize in local news. Complete assignments and research leads for newsworthy stories. Interview local government officials, corporate officers, community activists, business owners. Developed the series "On Your Block" for the weekend edition, featuring various local communities. Developed a five-part story exploring community relations of Illinois corporate businesses.

Education Reporter, *Honolulu Star-Bulletin,* 1979-1985.
Started as proofreader, within a year had written several feature stories, and within two years, obtained responsibility to research and report all education news.

Selected List of Publications

"Hadley & Hadley's Scramble for Community Support"
"Community Coalition: A Homegrown Response to Woes"
"Volunteerism: A Way of Life at Wright Brothers"
"Hawaii's Schools: Rebuilding Promises"
"Amelia Hunani: A New Breed of Administrator"
"Tea and Crumpets in the Southeast District"
"Evanston's Four-story Community: A Look at North Broadway"
"Revitalization: How Upscaling Affects Uptown Residents"
"WESTSTAR's Model Community Enrichment Program"

Education   Bachelor of Arts, Journalism and Government, University of Hawaii at Manoa, Honolulu.

References and Publication Portfolio on Request

Tanya Stewart
325 Matney Street
West Village, Utah 84872
(801) 555-7151

Career Objective	To bring my extensive communications background to the public relations department of a mid-sized West Coast computer products manufacturer.
Related Skills and Experience	Developed and produced a prototype newsletter to be distributed among alumni of the College of Science at Brigham Young University. Conducted reader survey to determine market interest and gather information relevant to the publication. Supervised continued publication of the newsletter. Responded to queries from readers.
	Conducted seminars on writing for publication for scientists and other technical professionals.
	Designed and instituted courses in technical writing and communication for science and engineering majors.
	Managed all institutional correspondence and communication with news media.
	Worked closely with public relations office of the university in developing news stories about scientific work conducted by university faculty in my college.
	Widely published in scientific and technical journals. Published two textbooks on scientific method in computer-aided investigation.
	Worked with science correspondents of major medical journals on the reporting of significant developments in cancer research at a medical laboratory under my direct supervision.
Employment History	Associate Dean, College of Science, Brigham Young University, Provo, Utah, 1985 to present Professor of Science, 1980 to present Associate Professor, 1977 to 1980 Assistant Professor, 1974 to 1977
	Director of Research, Mentor Laboratories, Salt Lake City, Utah, 1969 to 1974 Research Scientist, 1963 to 1965
Education	Postdoctoral Fellow, Cancer Research Unit, Bethlehem Children's Hospital, Maryland, 1972 to 1974 Doctorate, Chemistry, University of Wisconsin-Milwaukee, 1968 Bachelor of Science, Chemistry, University of Miami, Florida, 1965
	Publications list and references are available on request

Judd Riley, Jr.
P.O. Box 1254
Sioux Falls, South Dakota 57103
605-555-3828

Job Objective	Customer Service Department managerial position.

**Experience &
Achievements**

- *Customer Service/Public Relations*
  Direct interaction with clients and the public.
  Assess needs and provide solutions to customer
  complaints. Assist in product inquiries and setting up
  discounting programs for qualified customers.
  Represent company at trade shows. Utilize strong
  product knowledge in handling customer complaints
  through analysis and evaluation of complaint report.
  Support for sales force and on-site technicians.

- *Sales & Marketing*
  Assisted marketing research projects and conducted a
  general management survey for mini-warehouse
  industry. Coordinated promotional campaigns,
  utilizing database analysis to focus on target market.
  Responsible for selecting, ordering, and promoting the
  sales of sportswear to achieve over $125,000 in sales
  over a six-month period. Demonstrated skills in
  leadership, organization, and group motivation.
  Supervised sales staff of fourteen. Sold custom-made
  sportswear. Examined and evaluated markets through
  on-site observations and informal interviews.
  Supervised two employees.

**Employment
History**

Assistant Director, Public Relations
Morris Brothers, Sioux Falls, 1987-present

Management/Marketing Assistant
S.D. Management Services, Inc., Sioux Falls, 1979-87.

Promotion Coordinator/Sales Representative
Athletics West, Sioux Falls, 1976-79.

Associate Sales Manager
Danken Jewelers, Sioux Falls, 1973-75.

Education

B.A., 1973, Business and Marketing, University of Vermont,
Burlington

References

Will be forwarded upon request.

Darius G.W. Harms
3485 Plainfield Road
Lincoln, Nebraska 68573
402-555-9287

Career Goal	A POSITION IN ENGINEERING MANAGEMENT IN THE PUBLIC SECTOR

Achievements & Experience

- Supported construction and operating personnel during installation, start-up and testing of propulsion generator and hydraulic machinery.

- Performed facility survey, prepared technical reports, and provided engineering support during construction, start-up, and testing of the propulsion turbine plant.

- Directed structural and mechanical equipment development and operations.

- Coordinated fabrication and installation of full-size mock-up for integrated sub-base turbo generator.

- Provided support to designers, draftsmen, and construction personnel to ensure compliance with technical specifications and code requirements.

- Designed various mechanical and fluid systems and assisted in procurement, installation, and testing of systems and equipment.

- Designed and assisted in construction and testing of a flow-through crude oil handling system on oil recycler, reducing initial cost and increasing operational efficiency.

- Conducted equipment and system test at the factory and after site installation of various recycling components, including pumps, heat exchangers, hydraulics, and control/monitoring devices.

- Assisted in installation and testing of bulk petrochemical heating system.

- Assisted during installation, start-up, and testing of machinery for fiber, film cellulose, bulk material, and processing equipment.

- Developed and assisted in installation of automated overhead conveying system to replace manual material handling operation for cellulose sheet.

- Supervised installation of the filling line to increase bagging output for micro crystalline cellulose.

- Redesigned the PVC blown film machine and provided assistance during installation and start-up. Supervised a work force of 120 with responsibility over production and maintenance of oxygen and acetylene plant and facilities.

- Conducted the economic analysis for relocating oxygen plant. Supervised erection of the plant at the new site.

- Designed and assisted in the fabrication of the filtering system for acetylene. Supervised start-up and the testing of the system.

- Developed the test procedure for high pressure cylinders to meet regulatory requirements.

Work History

1988-1993 **Benton Recycling Machinery, Inc.,** Lincoln, Nebraska
Senior Engineer

1979-1988 **Taber Manufacturing,** Lincoln, Nebraska
Engineering Supervisor

1965-1979 **Tutwiller Bond Oxygen Corp, Ltd.,** Topeka, Kansas
Staff Engineer, Maintenance Engineer, Technician

Education   M.S., Mechanical Engineering, 1971, University of Kansas
B.S., Mechanical Engineering, 1965, University of Nebraska-Lincoln

References on request

Trina W. Vashon

122 Avenue of the Americas ➤ New York, New York 10015 ➤ 212/555-0933 (voice & fax)

Career Goal: Advertising Director for a small but growing New York agency.

EMPLOYMENT

Opera News, New York, New York
Director of Advertising, 9/88 to present
Advertising Sales, 6/82 to 9/88

➤ Handle distribution, retail marketing, advertising, and mail order marketing for monthly arts magazine.
➤ Schedule placement of advertising in publication according to advertisers' specifications.
➤ Handle all sales presentations to major advertising clients.
➤ Supervise staff of three advertising sales representatives.
➤ Direct weekly meetings with sales staff to plan sales strategies and track results of campaign efforts.

WREZ-FM Radio, Buffalo, New York
Marketing and Promotions Director, 5/77 to 6/80
Promotions Assistant, 3/76 to 5/77

➤ Assisted marketing director with radio and television promotion and retail marketing.
➤ Supervised staff of three full-time and seven part-time advertising sales representatives.
➤ Coordinated radio and print interview opportunities for visiting artists and writers.
➤ Directed research department for market data and sales reports.

Jones New York, New York
Marketing Department, 6/72 to 3/76

➤ Developed and implemented print and broadcast advertising campaign for major clothing manufacturer.

Education

University of New York, Buffalo
➤ Graduate study in Advertising and Marketing, 9/80 to 6/82
➤ Bachelor of Science in Journalism/Public Relations, 6/72

References upon request

PROFESSIONAL RESUME   DR. MARVIN A. ROBINSON

Office: (205) 555-3928   Home: (205) 555-3346
4483 Buck Drive   89 Fairview Place
Huntsville, Alabama 35804   Huntsville, Alabama 35804

OBJECTIVE | A managerial position with state government in which I may put my experience and skills in administration to best use

EDUCATION | Ph.D., University of Iowa, School Administration, 1975
M.S., Louisiana State University, Baton Rouge, Secondary Education, 1966
B.S., Louisiana State University, Elementary Education, 1964

EMPLOYMENT | Superintendent, Huntsville Schools, Alabama, 1988-present
Superintendent, Park School District, Prattsville, Alabama, 1980-1987
Principal, Mission High School, Montgomery, Alabama, 1975-1980
Principal, Jackson Heights Public Schools, Jackson, Alabama, 1973-1975
Assistant Principal, Jackson High School, Jackson, Alabama, 1970-1973
Math Teacher, Hopewell High School, Mobile, Alabama, 1966-1970

SELECTED AFFILIATIONS | Alabama Association of School Administrators
American Association of School Administrators
State Superintendent's Advisory Committee
State Department Evaluation Committee
Chamber of Commerce
Jobs Plus, Board of Directors
Leadership Development Program, Huntsville School District and University of Alabama
Louisiana State University, Graduate Instructor
University of Alabama, Graduate Instructor

SPEAKING ENGAGEMENTS AND CONSULTING PROJECTS | Baton Rouge, Louisiana, National Association of Secondary School Principals, "A Climate for Learning"
Toronto, Ontario, National Association of Secondary School Principals, "The School Administrator Under Stress"
National Academy for School Executives, Keynote speaker, "Educational Accountability: Three Approaches"
Individually Guided Education (IGE), Keynote Speaker
Louisiana Reading Association, Keynote Speaker
Alabama Librarians Association, Keynote Speaker
Missouri School Administrators Association, "Partnerships Between Districts and Businesses"

PUBLICATIONS | "The Road to Being a Superintendent," NASSP Bulletin
"Looking to the Future in American Education," ERIC
"Educational Approaches in Black High Schools," Alabama State Department Publication

HONORS | Talladega College, Member, Board of Trustees
Huntsville Chamber of Commerce, "Outstanding Educator Award 1987"
Louisiana State University
President, Black Student Union; Who's Who in American Colleges and Universities

REFERENCES AVAILABLE ON REQUEST

LANE TYLER
1892 Red River Road
Toledo, Ohio 43601
(419) 555-2078

Objective: A position as Instructor of Business and Marketing

Education:
M.B.A., 1992   Ohio University, Athens
B.A., 1969   State University of NY at Buffalo

Professional Experience:

1988-1990   **Director of Marketing,** Business Unit Leader, Foodservice
Pillar Paper Company, Toledo, Ohio
Responsibilities: Strategic and marketing leadership with profit
and loss accountability for a $310 million commercial
foodservice business. Develop a competitively advantaged
business by providing distinctive marketing, products, and
services that support customer and operator needs. Direct
development of environmental strategies for paper products.
Provide manufacturing with objectives and standards for raw
material sourcing, quality improvement, and cost reduction.
Lead business planning process.
Accomplishments: Increased division earnings by 17 percent in
1989. Initiated a new products development program. Introduced
operator-focused marketing programs to pull product through
distribution.

1986-1988   **Senior Marketing Manager,** Commercial Products Division
Responsibilities: Led development and marketing of new high
performance products and systems for towels and soaps.
Developed and led a foodservice venture for the Commercial
Products division. Managed integration efforts with the
Foodservice Corporation. With sales management, developed
target market strategies.
Accomplishments: Lead development and marketing of a new
towel brand which contributed over $1 million in new earnings
within eighteen months. The foodservice venture generated $2
million incremental earnings in 1988. Awarded one of three
Business Excellence awards for my contributions in 1987-1988.

1983-1985   **Senior Marketing Manager,** Foodservice Division
Responsibilities: Directed marketing and development for 650
foodservice products. Developed foodservice strategies that
aligned with commercial towel and tissue business objectives.
Directed Marketing Communications programs.
Accomplishments: Improved Specialty Products earnings by 10
percent in 1984 and 1985 with a balance of marketing programs
and price guideline development.

1980-1983   **Director of Marketing and Sales**, American Convenience, Inc.,
               Toledo, Ohio
               Responsibilities: Reported to the President and directed all sales
               and marketing functions, with accountability for continuous
               earnings improvement. Responsible for product and program
               development, advertising, customer service, and a twenty-five
               person sales staff.
               Accomplishments: Initiated a national accounts program.
               Introduced American's first sales incentive program which
               helped drive a 12 percent increase in sales and profits in the first
               year.

1975-1980   **Group Products Manager**, American Convenience, Inc.
               Responsibilities: Accountable for management of all product
               lines toward profitable growth. Managed promotion, product
               design, advertising, forecasting, and pricing. Planned all national
               and regional trade show representation.
               Accomplishments: Led development of Spectrum Colors
               promotional program which significantly altered the way the
               industry markets color napkins.

1969-1975   **Branch Sales Manager**, Time-Life Books, Pittsburgh,
               Pennsylvania
               Responsibilities: Staffed, organized, and managed the first branch
               sales office in the Eastern U.S. Developed and managed testing
               for retail distribution of our products.
               Accomplishments: Developed sales training manual for all
               branches. Initiated WATS line concept of national selling and
               reduction of sales costs.

References Provided on Request

Jerold M. Short
3554 Front Street #306
Gallup, New Mexico 87321
505/555-2283

Career Ambition: Teaching and Research Position with a Major Medical Center or Hospital

Related Experience:

Good Samaritan Hospital
Gallup, New Mexico
Emergency Room Registered Nurse
(January 1980 to present)

- Trained new emergency room nurses and technicians with appropriate ER procedures.
- Triaged all incoming patients and worked with EMT staff to stabilize patients.
- Assisted physicians with suturing and casting.
- Administered IVs and medications.
- Provided emergency medical care, including CPR.
- Supervised nursing staff of emergency rooms during night and weekend shifts.

Central Albuquerque Community Hospital
Albuquerque, New Mexico
ICU/CCU Registered Nurse
(January 1977 to November 1979)

- Supervised nursing staff on weekends.
- Coordinated nursing and lay teams in providing emotional and psychological support for terminal patients and their families.
- Monitored temporary pacemakers; assisted with insertion of intra-aortic balloon pumps; interpreted 12-lead electrocardiograms; inserted catheters and IVs; assisted doctors with examinations and administered required medications; assisted with cardioversions.
- Instructed outpatients recovering from open-heart surgery and myocardial infarction.

Buck Ambulance
Albuquerque, New Mexico
Emergency Medical Technician
(September 1972 to January 1975)

- Responded to emergency calls for medical assistance.
- Triaged patients on site and prepared for transportation to hospital or medical center facilities.
- Assisted hospital medical personnel in transfer of patients and emergency room care.
- Administered IVs and various types of emergency medical intervention.

Education:

RN, University of Santa Fe, New Mexico, 1977
EMT, University of Santa Fe, New Mexico, 1971

Memberships: Sigma Theta Tau (National honor society for nursing), American Association of Critical Care Nurses, National Hospice Nurses Association, American Heart Association Volunteer Instructor, American Red Cross Volunteer Instructor.

References available on request

KEVIN FOXWORTH
2114 Renton Street
Kirkland, Washington 98005
206/555-3497

CAREER OBJECTIVE — Engineering position with industrial manufacturing company.

CAPABILITIES

• Manage continuous fire furnaces that produce flat pressed glass and glass for machine and hand blowing.

• Plan and supervise all aspects of furnace operation and maintenance, including personnel scheduling and staffing.

• Evaluate alternative production methods and materials to reduce costs and improve product quality.

• Control raw materials inventory, ordering, and inspection.

• Train employees in use and maintenance of equipment.

• Review product availability and equipment developments to keep systems up-to-date for both production and safety concerns.

• Plan, coordinate, and supervise all aspects of glassware production.

ACHIEVEMENTS

• Initiated improved method for raw materials handling that resulted in $250,000 in actual savings.

• Worked with production engineers to develop new heating procedures that made furnaces 20 percent more efficient in start-up time.

• Developed operating procedures that improved worker safety.

• Designed alternative casing that reduced external temperatures dramatically, thus decreasing fire and burn hazard.

• Given Award of Merit for developing material composition that produced greater clarity in pressed glass products.

WORK HISTORY

1975 - present	Pilchuck GlassWorks Factory, Seattle, Washington Furnace/Production Manager
1964 - 1975	Boeing, Renton, Washington Senior Technician, Instrumentation Casing Section

EDUCATION

1988	BS, Engineering, University of Washington
1963	AA, Technology & Industry Production, Everett Community College, Everett, Washington

REFERENCES — Available when requested.

DAVID SAMUELS
84 BAYONET STREET
CHATTANOOGA, TENNESSEE 37401
(615) 555-9388

SUMMARY: Sales and Marketing Manager who wishes to enter the Publishing Industry as Sales Representative or in Sales Management. Proven leadership ability to conceptualize, structure, and achieve both market and profit objectives.

PROFESSIONAL EXPERIENCE:

National Sales Manager, Washington Paper, Subsidiary of PaperGraphics, Inc., Chattanooga, TN, 1984-present
- Assumed total responsibility for sales of commodity and specialty papers in the U.S. and Canada with total sales in excess of $50 million.
- Coordinated with manufacturing the transfer of specialty paper manufacturing to another mill. Upgraded that mill from commodity to specialty paper producer.
- Created and implemented the Neighborhood Business Strategy, concentrating sales efforts to develop business close to the mill, effectively reducing costs and improving profitability.
- Initiated sales incentive program to motivate the sales force to generate new product sales.
- Initiated aggressive sales efforts for additional volume, allowing increased production, using idle equipment which spread costs and substantially improved profits.

Sales Manager, Repro-paper, Inc., Subsidiary of PaperGraphics, Inc., Buffalo, NY, 1975-1984
- Held responsibility for sales of all copy-type papers, which represented 40 percent of sales.
- Directed department of six sales professionals.
- Reduced dependence on major accounts by expanding customer base and raising prices.
- Improved profitability stressing quality, service, and elimination of volume price contracts which were depressing profits.
- Changed company image perception from volume supplier to top-quality product producer dedicated to customer service.
- Supported our customers through National Trade and Industry Association participation.

Product Manager, Specialty Papers, Greenfield Paper Company, Subsidiary of PaperGraphics, Inc., Greenfield, MA, 1972-1975
- Assumed newly created position, established its function, and made it work profitably.
- Established specifications, pricing, and developed marketing strategies.
- Consolidated product lines in Greeting Card, Wallpaper, and Copy paper markets.
- Developed trade names, product identification, and customer recognition.
- Implemented advertising campaigns with assistance from ad agencies.
- Worked with Technical Department to develop Technical Bulletins and supporting materials in the Greeting Card, Wallpaper, Photographic, and Flameproof markets.
- Worked closely with regional salesmen and their customers to develop greater product use and customer satisfaction.

Salesman, Greenfield Paper Company, 1963-1972
- Increased sales from $250,000 to $600,000 in the first year.
- Successfully built sales to over $3,000,000 by 1972.
- Recognized as especially proficient in developing new customers.

EDUCATION:
- B.S., Business, University of Pittsburgh, Pennsylvania, 1963.

REFERENCES AVAILABLE UPON REQUEST

Lucille Sirois
392 Altura Drive • Geneva, Illinois 60134
Home (708) 555-8372 • Work (312) 555-3846

OBJECTIVE

Advertising staff of a major international publishing house. Particularly interested in a position that will utilize my written and verbal fluency in German.

PROFESSIONAL EXPERIENCE

Berlin America, Chicago, IL. Manager and Buyer, 1988-current.

- Develop, produce, and implement direct mail and newspaper advertising campaigns that have directly contributed to a 45 percent sales growth over four years.
- Buy and merchandise German textile and ceramic hand-crafted items.
- Maintain financial control of $375,000 annual sales volume.
- Translate business-related documents German-English/English-German.

Books, Etc., Bookstore, Minneapolis, MN. Manager / Regional Planner, 1984-1988.

- Responsible for effective visual presentation for three area stores.
- Trained and supervised ten employees.
- Controlled inventory and financial planning of $300,000 annual sales volume.

La France, Edina, MN. Counter Manager, 1980-1984.

- Supervised staff of twelve waiters.
- Supervised food preparation and distribution.
- Integrated daily cash receipts into restaurant financial budget.

KSMR Radio, Collegeville, MN. Assistant Director of Programming, 1976-1979. News Announcer/DJ, 1974-1976.

- Hired and scheduled staff of 25 volunteer disc jockeys.
- Implemented listener survey which increased funding by 63 percent.
- Wrote and engineered news programming and public service announcements.

EDUCATION

St. John's University, Collegeville, MN.
- Bachelor of Arts in Government and German, awarded 1984.

Institute for American Universities, Berlin, Germany.
- German language coursework, 1988.

REFERENCES AVAILABLE

FAITH NUYGEN ◆ 775 S.W. Tilbury Road ◆ Fresno, California 93723 ◆ (209) 555-7623

CAREER OBJECTIVE: Project Management Director

EXPERIENCE

Communications Manager, Consortium of California Counties, Fresno, 1983 - present
The Consortium administers an annual federal grant of $25 million for employment and training programs in 35 counties. As the first Communications Manager of the Administrative Office, I developed and implemented a public relations effort for the Job Training Partnership Act (JTPA).
> *Highlights:*
> ◆ Develop annual report, newsletter, brochures, and other materials to market program's job training services to private business, public sector, and job seekers.
> ◆ Received National Business Alliance Distinguished Performance Award.
> ◆ Conceived and managed a statewide conference for employment and training professionals; hosted visiting International Fellowship representatives from four European countries.
> ◆ Directed work of advertising agency and support staff.
> ◆ Coordinated communications among various branches and county offices.
> ◆ Designed and maintained systems for recruiting, selecting, and training members of the Private Industry Association of California and local elected officials of the CCC Board of Directors. Managed quarterly meetings and biannual retreat.
> ◆ Supervised effort to diversify funding resources for the CCC.
> ◆ Coordinated multi-media job seeker recruitment campaign sold in 26 states.
> ◆ Responsible for tracking state and federal legislation with potential impact on CCC programs. Prepared testimony and information for legislators. Attended state legislative hearings.

Risk Manager, Consortium of California Counties, Fresno, 1981 - 1983
Developed and implemented risk management system to assure limitation of program risks and compliance with federal and state laws. Served as liaison to district branch offices and state, regional, and federal offices of the Department of Labor in the interpretation and implementation of laws and regulations.
> *Highlights:*
> ◆ Developed system of procedures to identify and monitor program risks.
> ◆ Conducted comprehensive Risk Management Reviews of districts for compliance with state and federal laws.
> ◆ Responsible for development, training, and implementation of EEO/AA policy and Affirmative Action Plan. Investigated and processed complaints.
> ◆ Developed grievance procedure and trained all CCC managers statewide.

Personnel Director, International Paper Suppliers, San Francisco, 1972 - 1976
Responsible for Industrial Relations functions and monitoring EEO/AA activities for a corporation with 95 corporate locations nationwide. First woman in the corporation's history to hold this position. (Hired in Corporate Communications Department in 1968).
> *Highlights:*
> ◆ Interpreted and administered labor contract and represented the company in local and master bargaining.
> ◆ Developed corporate policy manual on EEO/AA. Designed a brochure for corporate use and conducted regional EEO/AA seminars in corporate supervisory training courses.
> ◆ Coordinated corporate community programs.
> ◆ Worked with field managers to prepare for government regulations compliance review.

EDUCATION

B.A. in Communications, Stanford University, 1968

Portfolio and references available on request.

Joseph W. Caldwell
346 Buena Vista
Pocatello, Idaho 83251
(208) 555-6682

Job Goal: Construction Foreman for Housing Construction Company

Skills: Experienced in a wide range of construction and wood
                 products occupations.
                 Thorough knowledge of indigenous woods and their
                 suitability for construction.
                 Twenty years of supervisory experience.

Work History: Supervisor, Twin Peaks Plywood, Pocatello
                 Trained and supervised millworkers in all areas of mill
                 operation. Scheduled shifts of 24 workers each, three
                 shifts a day. Worked relief schedule on weekends.
                 Developed safety awareness program. Monitored safety
                 procedures. Consulted with SAIF inspectors for methods
                 of improving working environment safety. Employed
                 continuously from 1978 to January 1993 (mill shut
                 down).

                 Shift Foreman, Idaho Lumber Supply, Boise
                 Supervised splitters, pullers, and saw operators on day
                 shift. Trained workers in all aspects of lumber mill
                 operation. Monitored safety procedures. Employed
                 initially as mill worker; worked seasonally from 1972
                 to 1978 (moved).

                 Carpentry Crewman, Dales Construction, Boise
                 Worked on carpentry crew building residential dwellings
                 and office complexes in Boise and environs. Experienced
                 with foundation work, roofing, sheetrocking, and finish
                 carpentry. Worked seasonally from 1969 to 1978 (moved).

                 Woodworker, Ames Oak Furniture, Boise
                 Operated lathe, power saw, miter saw, drill press,
                 scroll saw, burnishing sander, and other power
                 equipment in the manufacture and finishing of solid oak
                 furniture. Employed full-time from 1967 to 1969
                 (business relocated out of state).

Education: Boise Central High School, 1967

Memberships: International Millworkers Local #655
                 Carpenter's Local #2815
                 American Woodworkers Association
                 Northwest Timber Workers Association
                 Boise Sportsmen's Association
                 Boise Lions Club, Membership Secretary, 1989
                 Pocatello Boys & Girls Club, Volunteer Coach

                 Licensed and Bonded - References available

Janet Lee Kosh
2314 Sunnyview Drive, N.W.
Springfield, Missouri 65812
417/555-9076

Professional Objective: Seeking new challenges in a position as communications director in a private-sector corporate environment.

Previous Experience:

Director of Communications, City of Springfield, October 1981 to present
  Plan and direct public information program for the City of Springfield.
  Supervise city management communications with the general public and corporate
    representatives.
  Coordinate writing, design, and production of city's annual report to taxpayers, newsletter to local
    businesses and the chamber of commerce members, and brochures covering important
    aspects of city planning.
  Consult with business leaders, civic leaders, and public arts organizations on fund-raising
    programs for community-wide projects.

Director of Communications, Office of Development, Washington University, St. Louis, 1973 to 1980
  Plan development communications strategies and programs for corporate, individual, and alumni
    fund-raising efforts.
  Direct public information program: write and distribute press releases and feature articles,
    coordinate and secure necessary design services, plan and develop new public information
    and publication projects as needs are identified.
  Respond to information requests from the general public, university faculty and students, and
    alumni.
  Coordinate inter-departmental fund-raising tracking system and communications.

Publications Coordinator, Cartwright/Haeuser/Martinez Architects, St. Louis, 1968 to 1973
  Write, edit, and submit articles to professional and trade journals; prepare entries for architectural
    awards programs.
  Maintain project books and photo and slide files for use in client presentations.
  Develop presentation graphics; contract with designers.
  Produce general office graphic materials, including 240-page promotional book.

Honors & Awards:
  Gold Award, Two-Color Publications, CASE National, 1973
  Silver Award, One-Color Publications, CASE National, 1972
  Gold Award, Capital Campaign, CASE National, 1972

Education:
  Bachelor of Arts, Graphic Design/Writing (dual major), Washington University, 1965

Continuing Education Conferences & Workshops:
  Design and Communications for Corporate Publications, Dallas, Texas, 1992
  City Managers Association Conference, annually, 1981-1992
  PageMaker Workshop, Apple Computer, Inc., Springfield, 1991
  Getting Things Done, CareerTrack Seminar, Vancouver, B.C., Canada, 1991
  Desktop Publishing Seminar, Publish Magazine, San Francisco, California, 1990
  CASE Conference on Capital Campaign Communications, Indianapolis, Indiana, 1971

References and portfolio furnished upon request

NORTON W. WALTERS

10563 S.E. Powell Blvd., Tulsa, Oklahoma 74135 / (918) 555-4436

PERSONAL FOCUS

Financial analysis and strategic marketing management

PROFESSIONAL EXPERIENCE

Financial
Financial analysis, cash flow analysis, securities analysis, business and economic forecasting, and project feasibility studies

Marketing
Market analysis and testing, strategic planning and administration, market research, opinion polling and analysis, coordinating and facilitating focus groups

Management
Program and project management, staff supervision, budget preparation and administration, MIS reviews and management audits, public relations, staff development, personnel recruitment and selection, union contract interpretation and administration, Affirmative Action and EEO compliance planning and administration

Communication
Team building, employee relations counseling, dispute resolution and mediation, public speaking, report writing, group facilitation

CAREER PATH

President and CEO, Step One Enterprises, 1984 - 1992
Began international trading and brokerage corporation with affiliations in China, Hong Kong, Taiwan, and the Philippines. Sold business after achieving personal and professional goals.

Consultant, Various corporate and public sector clients, 1981 - present
Providing business consulting services in market analysis, marketing strategy and planning, public relations, budgeting and financial analysis.

Partner, Henderson, Walters, & Larsen, Business Consultants, 1980 - 1981
Principal in firm providing market analysis and planning, business forecasting, and financial analysis for private firms and nonprofit organizations.

Division Manager, State of Oklahoma, Employment and Human Services, 1968 - 1976
Managed job development and placement with a staff of 24. Conducted program evaluation and planning. Developed public relations program and hired personnel. Served as liaison to Governor's office for employment issues.

EDUCATION

Master of Business Administration, Finance and Management
University of California, Berkeley, 1980

Bachelor of Arts, Philosophy
University of Colorado, Boulder, 1966

References furnished upon request

JANE P. HARPER
8395 Beaumont Drive
Lincoln, Nebraska 68508
(402) 555-3948

OBJECTIVE: A management position in a major Midwest private corporation that will maximize my proven abilities in:

- **Administrative Management**
- **Organizational Development**
- **Corporate Affairs**
- **Public and Community Relations**

SKILLS / EXPERIENCE

- Recruited, trained, and developed management teams of up to 15, supervising up to 2,800 employees.
- Successfully prepared and administered operating and capital budgets totaling up to $133 million.
- Experienced in initiating and overseeing all operating functions associated with capital improvement projects totaling $150 million.
- Developed marketing and public relations programs that generated significant private-sector business. Created public and private-sector partnerships that fostered substantial commercial and entrepreneurial growth.
- Guided operations analyses resulting in significant efficiency improvements and cost savings through changes in work processes and operating procedures, upgrades to management methods and systems, and reallocation and down-sizing of work force.

CAREER HISTORY

Chief Executive Officer
City of Lincoln
- Recruited in 1986 to improve the financial situation, strengthen organizational planning and development as well as establish better communication and information management systems. Responsible for administrative and business affairs including management staffing, budgeting, finance, employee relations, service programs, and community relations.
- Initiated multi-level operations analysis used as basis for creating new strategic plan.
- Identified and led planning, design, and completion of capital improvement projects totaling more than $150 million.
- Supervised development of business plan that reduced operating costs $800,000 in key corporate component.
- Initiated analysis and guided development of internal organization to better manage labor relations and employee benefits functions. Eliminated two-year backlog of unresolved worker compensation cases.

JANE P. HARPER
Page 2

- Prepared and implemented reorganization that resulted in creation of central data processing and management information services functions.
- Lead city's involvement with private business sector to support new economic base expansion plan and public/private marketing organization.

General Manager
City of Greeley, Colorado
- Recruited in 1984 to unify and upgrade administrative systems/procedures and gain better control of finances. Responsible for all day-to-day operations.
- Introduced coordinated management reporting system which yielded significant improvements in internal/external communications, management decision-making, and organizational efficiency.
- Adapted existing budget to modified zero-base budgeting system.
- Reversed trend of economic base erosion by working with existing businesses to foster expansion and improved competitiveness.

Previous Experience: Includes progressive general management positions in public-sector organizations in Florida, Oklahoma, and Maine.

EDUCATION

Master's Degree, Marcus Graduate School, University of Ohio, Athens, 1980
Bachelor's Degree, Bates College, Lewiston, Maine , 1975

References provided on request

ADRIAN KASIMOR
389 NORTH BEND
IOWA CITY, IOWA 52240
(319) 555-2243

OBJECTIVE:

A position involved in the Management of a Conference Center or Conference Services

EXPERIENCE

Assistant Director, U of
Iowa Summer Quarter,
1980-present
University of Iowa
Iowa City

- Direct administrative operations, U of Iowa Summer Quarter.
- Make policy decisions and direct long-range planning.
- Responsible for program development and communications with vice presidents, academic deans, department chairs, and academic unit personnel.
- Manage the development, preparation, justification of budgets and accounting operations.
- Direct marketing and publicity campaign.

Conference
Administrator, 1975-80
University of Iowa
Iowa City

- Managed bi-annual international seminars.
- Produced brochures; made registration and site arrangements; developed and maintained operating budget.
- Coordinated additional conferences, seminars, workshops.

Administrative
Assistant, 1972-75
University of Iowa
Iowa City

- Managed/supervised Academic Records Department.
- Assisted in start-up operations of University conference and performing arts center.

EDUCATION

University of Iowa, Iowa City
B.A., Psychology, 1971
Other Courses and Workshops:
- Supervision
- WordPerfect Desktop Publishing
- The New Supervisor / Manager
- Practical Ways to Improve Your Communication

REFERENCES

Available on request

Tucker Wendell
P.O. Box 12597
Cincinnati, Ohio 45204
513/555-9041

Objective

To continue my work with young people in a position as a vocational counselor in a program involved with at-risk or disadvantaged youth.

Experience	Skills
Hired and trained workers in a variety of positions with a food processing company.	Ability to work well with a wide range of people. Knowledge of job training and hiring procedures.
Supervised high school-age workers in fast food restaurant.	Understanding of work requirements and abilities of teenage workers.
Served as volunteer coordinator of annual jobs fair for high school students. Worked with business people, professionals, and employers to develop program directed to high school students for career planning and preparation.	Developed understanding of employer needs and expectations in local job market. Ability to counsel students on job demands and opportunities. Developed contacts in the work world that could be invaluable to young people seeking job opportunities.
Assisted with summer camp and outdoor school programs for local school district. Taught woodworking segment at camp.	Ability to work with children of all ages, from elementary student campers to the high school students who worked as camp counselors.
Served as president of the Parent-Teacher Association.	Ability to work with parents to solve problems.

Employment History

Employment and Training Manager, Food-Pac Corporation, Cincinnati, Ohio
1985-present

Responsible for hiring and training line workers and shift supervisors in food processing company. Work with local employment agencies and high school and college counselors to find qualified individuals for specialty assignments. Handle employee performance evaluations. Developed reporting system to monitor productivity and established reward program.

Manager, Burger King Corporation, Store #1252
1975-1985

Hired and trained high school students and older workers for food preparation and cashier positions. Monitored sales reports. Scheduled shifts. Conducted employee performance reviews.

Related Volunteer Experience

President, West High School PTA
Coordinator, West School District Jobs Fair
Teacher/Counselor, Camp Arrawanna
Coach, Boys & Girls Club Soccer Program

References available upon request

Joella Baker • 3892 North Vista • Tucson, Arizona 85726 • 602-555-3828

Objective
A position in public relations or promotion that will utilize my organizational, communications, and planning skills.

Professional Experience

Office Manager, Health Consortium, Tucson, AZ, 1985-present

Organize and direct all company office activities, including: interviewing, selecting, training, scheduling, and supervising office support personnel; overseeing administration of employee benefits plans and assisting with claims. Assist in compliance to Arizona Safety Board reporting regulations.

Establish effective procedures and policies; oversee quality performance of customer service, public relations, and clerical activities; troubleshoot complex and/or sensitive customer problems. Plan work flow assignments to successfully meet all established deadlines and management objectives; interact effectively with all departments to provide highest levels of efficiency and to maintain excellent standards of customer service.

Assist Controller with cash management and other financial duties. Assist in banking negotiations and procedures pertinent to Chapter 11 status.

- *Proficient in use of IBM and compatible ACCPAC accounting and word processing systems and software.*

Credit & Collection Manager, Health Consortium, Tucson, AZ, 1981-85

Responsible for reviewing and verifying company credit applications and setting credit limits for clients. Developed and recommended appropriate changes in credit policy to management. Processed authorized orders, prepared invoices; credited account payments and tracked past due amounts. Sent late notices and negotiated customer payment arrangements for collection of delinquent account balances.

Customer Service Manager, Health Consortium, Tucson, AZ, 1975-81

Made direct contact with customers and prospective clients; maintained highest possible customer service standards. Maintained current knowledge of sales and special promotional events; served as support and backup for marketing/sales force. Provided customers with general and technical product information and special assistance. Promptly resolved order and/or account problems; ensured that orders were received; interacted effectively with other company departments; tracked order shipments through contact with freight company representatives.

Conducted customer research projects to determine amendments and/or new, improved features and service policies.

- *Selected to represent Health Consortium at key trade shows.*
- *Promoted to Credit and Collection Manager.*

Receptionist/Cost Accounting, Penobscot Wire & Cable, Everett, MA, 1973-74

Answered and directed incoming/outgoing switchboard calls; verified job cost information; performed daily calculations and maintained accurate and current bookkeeping records; responsible for miscellaneous typing assignments.

Sales/Office Support Staff, Brunswick River News, Everett, MA, 1970-73

Developed major promotional ideas for increasing print advertising revenues; coordinated sales of regular block and classified advertising sections. Served as personal liaison to advertising agencies in the Everett and Boston areas; made effective sales presentations and secured new accounts.

Maintained accounts receivable; made bank deposits; performed billing functions on Vector 9000 computer system. Assisted controller with collections activities and served as office receptionist.

- *Established successful 2-page advertising section for* Before School *promotion; initiated* Drive Slow *feature and* New England Antique Paper *advertising sections.*

Education & Training

B.A. Business Administration, University of Arizona, Tucson, AZ, 1991

General Studies, Tucson Community College, Tucson, AZ, 1978-79

References Available on Request

JEFFERSON BIRD
3829 HIGH ROAD
WARWICK, RI 02887
401 555-9287

OBJECTIVE	A POSITION IN ENGINEERING MANAGEMENT IN THE PUBLIC SECTOR
BACKGROUND SUMMARY	Over twenty years experience in construction and mechanical engineering for private corporations, specifically: field engineer for installation of propulsion turbine plant on land-based test site; industrial and product engineering in the shipbuilding, material handling, chemical, and gas industries in construction, maintenance, engineering, and administrative capacities.
EDUCATION	M.S., Mechanical Engineering, 1969, Eastern University, Springfield, MA B.S., Mechanical Engineering, 1965, Pennsylvania Institute of Technology, Pittsburgh, PA

EXPERIENCE
1982-1992

Newport Shipbuilders, Inc., Warwick, RI
Senior Engineer
- Supported construction and operating personnel during installation, start-up, and testing of propulsion, generator, and hydraulic machinery.
- Performed facility survey, prepared technical reports, and provided engineering support during construction, start-up, and testing of the propulsion turbine plant.
- Assisted in construction during structural and mechanical equipment support and foundation.
- Coordinated fabrication and installation of full size mock-up for integrated sub-base turbo generator.
- Provided support to designers, draftsmen, and construction personnel to ensure compliance with technical specifications and code requirements.

1974-1982

Shipbuilders Corporation, Providence, RI
Engineering Supervisor
- Designed various mechanical and fluid systems and assisted in procurement, installation, and testing of systems and equipment.
- Designed and assisted in construction and testing of a flow-through crude oil handling system on 120,000 ton double-hull tanker, reducing initial cost and increasing operational efficiency.
- Organized a multi-disciplinary team to develop and build an oil-water separator to meet pollution control requirements.
- Conducted equipment and system test at the factory and after completion of installation for various components, including pumps, heat exchangers, hydraulics, and control/monitoring devices.
- Assisted in installation and testing of bulk petrochemical heating system to maintain the product temperature.

1969-1973   **TEC, Fiber Division**, Boston, MA
Staff Engineer
- Assisted during installation, start-up, and testing of machinery for fiber, film cellulose, and bulk material and processing equipment.
- Developed and assisted in installation of automated overhead conveying system to replace manual material handling operation for cellulose sheet.
- Supervised installation of the filling line to increase bagging output for micro crystalline cellulose.
- Redesigned the PVC blown film machine and provided assistance during installation and start-up.

1965-1967   **Pennsylvania Oxygen Corp, Ltd.**, Pittsburgh, PA
Assistant Engineer
- Supervised a work force of 120 with responsibility over production and maintenance of oxygen and acetylene plant and facilities.
- Conducted the economic analysis for relocating oxygen plant. Supervised erection of the plant at the new site.
- Designed and assisted in the fabrication of the filtering system for acetylene. Supervised start-up and the testing of the system.
- Developed the test procedure for high pressure cylinders to meet regulatory requirements.

REFERENCES ON REQUEST

STUART DAVID MARKS

66-B W. 45th Street • Wilmington, Delaware 19835 • 302 - 555-8223

PROFESSIONAL OBJECTIVE

To bring my extensive experience as a certified public accountant into the administration of a large metropolitan arts organization.

EDUCATION

University of Chicago • MBA, 1975
Emphasis in Finance and Accounting

Illinois State University • BS, Business, 1970
Emphasis in Accounting

WORK EXPERIENCE

Corporate Accounting Department Manager, Bowles and Sharp, CPA • 1979 to present

• Direct staff of twenty-seven certified public accountants and fifteen support staff.

• Responsible for all corporate accounts, valued at more than $7.5 billion.

• Serve as liaison between accounting department and corporate CEOs.

• Reduced losses through implementation of cost accounting controls for two major corporate clients.

• Supervise corporate audits and hold final responsibility for federal and state reporting.

• Develop and maintain strategic corporate plans and accounting division budgets.

• Review and work with agency management to develop and monitor corporate plans and goals.

Certified Public Accountant, Tarrant Michaels & Associates, Inc. • 1975 to 1979

• Handled ongoing accounting and reporting for twenty-five corporate clients.

• Prepared corporate and individual federal income tax reports.

• Audited corporate and public organization finances.

• Prepared financial statements for credit reporting and bank financing.

MEMBERSHIPS

Certified Public Accountants of Delaware
National Association of Certified Public Accountants
Wilmington Chamber of Commerce Board of Directors • Treasurer, 1991 to present
Farmington County Arts Center Board of Directors • Vice President, Finance, 1988 to 1990

REFERENCES are available upon request

Donna Everson
1233 Mission Street
San Pablo, California 98329
212/555-0812

Goal	Obtain a sales or marketing position requiring analysis and strategic planning.

Education	Oregon State University, 1993
	  MBA, Marketing
	
	Massachusetts Institute of Technology, 1974
	  MS, Civil Engineering
	
	University of California, Los Angeles, 1972
	  BS, Engineering

Experience	CH2M Hill, Inc. 1985 - 1991 **Civil Engineer**

- Responsible for analysis and design of transportation systems.

- Coordinated planning and construction with city, state, and federal government engineers.

- Successfully negotiated contract for $26.8 million in highway construction for the city of Los Angeles.

- Responsible for developing cost-benefit ratios, staff and material estimates and schedules, and project budgets.

- Experienced with computer-aided design, drafting, and structural analysis.

Shell Oil Company
1975 - 1984
Engineering Sales Specialist

- Responsible for home heating oil sales program and technical support for distribution companies.

- Designed and implemented a marketing program for potential distributors that resulted in 23% increased sales over the previous year.

- Developed a network of technical support for both distributors and end-users of the product.

- Coordinated marketing and sales programs with heater manufacturers to stimulate sales in the small business market.

- Provided technical support to manufacturers and distributors for selecting appropriate weight and type of oil according to burner specifications.

Honors	Michaelson-Davis Award for Outstanding Contribution from a New Employee, 1986 Who's Who in Engineering, 1990 Chapter President, Society of Women Engineers, 1989 - 1991 Phi Kappa Phi Delta Upsilon Pi, Engineering Honorary
References	Available on request

Deanna Smith
3476 W. Seventh
Las Vegas, NV 89133
☎ (702) 555-4756

Career Goal
Director or Administrator position with government agency.

Achievements

☛ Direct administrative operations for college continuing education program.

☛ Make policy decisions with regard to operations management and communications.

☛ Responsible for long-range planning and program development.

☛ Liaison to department directors and college top administration.

☛ Manage development, preparation, and justification of accounting and budgeting operations.

☛ Coordinate annual international seminar, including registration, accommodations, travel and site arrangements, budgeting, and production of brochures.

☛ Supervised department of academic records.

☛ Coordinated conferences, seminars, and workshops with a variety of government and private organizations.

☛ Assisted in start-up operations of conference center.

☛ Experienced with corporate general ledger bookkeeping, auditing, payroll, and year-end closing.

☛ Experienced with credit management, credit reviews, and collections.

Employment Experience
Assistant Director, Continuing Education, University of Nevada, Las Vegas, 1989-present
Conference Center Associate Administrator, UNLV Conference Center, 1981-present
Management Assistant, Continuing Education, UNLV, 1985-89
Assistant to the Director, Continuing Education, UNLV, 1983-85
Administrative Assistant, Continuing Education, UNLV, 1981-83
Secretary, Continuing Education, UNLV, 1979-81
Corporate Accounting, Miller & Sherwin, Engineering Associates, Las Vegas, 1977-79
Accounts Receivable, Caesar's Palace, Las Vegas, 1972-76

Education
B.A. Business Administration, 1989
Las Vegas Business College, Office Management, 1972

References available as requested

DAVID J. MASTERS
169 W. Broad Street
Concord, New Hampshire 03301
603/555-3948

CAREER OBJECTIVE

    Marketing Associate with Advertising Department of Major Retailer

EDUCATION

    Continuing Education Coursework, Concordia College   *1991 to 1992*
    Business courses in marketing, management, and advertising

    Bachelor of Science, Library Science, Boston University   *1965*

EMPLOYMENT RECORD

    Research and Development Specialist, Public Relations Department,
    New Hampshire Job Training Program, Concord   *1978 to present*

    Provide job market consulting services, prepare program proposals and
    contracts, coordinate activities with consultants, and handle customer service.
    Complete study of present and future needs of the administrative unit and
    district offices, including capability of service delivery based on anticipated
    funding. Draft and implement a plan for research and development activities,
    with primary emphasis on identifying funding sources. Develop and maintain
    computerized resource library of publications, market surveys, books, studies,
    videos, training programs, and individual resources. Supervise staff of seven;
    serve as liaison to county offices.

    Research Librarian, Business and Technology Department, County Library,
    Concord, New Hampshire   *1970 to 1978*

    Maintained active records on resources for research in business and technology.
    Responded to queries from library patrons for research resources. Worked with
    individuals to develop research plans for using library resources. Remained
    current with new developments in the fields. Supervised staff of five.

    Associate Librarian, New Hampshire State Library, Concord   *1965 to 1970*

    Maintained all state, local, and federal government publications. Developed
    catalog of publications available at the state library facility. Supervised library
    interns in cataloging project for state library system.

REFERENCES

    Available on request.

ALICIA CARPENTIER ♦   3890 West Arlington • Syracuse, NY 13201 • (315) 555-3294

OBJECTIVE
A position as Music Department Director at a public high school.

HIGHLIGHTS OF QUALIFICATIONS

♦ Ten years as a private instrumental, voice, and music theory instructor.
♦ Founder and director of *Santos*, a Renaissance choral and instrumental group.
♦ Coordinated fundraising for the Arts Council: established goals, formulated policies, organized efforts.

RELATED ACTIVITIES

1981-current: Founded a performance group focused on Renaissance music. Coordinated extensive research on early instrumentation, authenticity of performance. Act as director, arrange scores, and organize performances for the nonprofit chorus, *Santos*.

1986 and 1987: Conductor of Student Orchestra, New York State Music Festival.

1975-1981: Member of Sacred Choir of Syracuse.

1972-1975: Member, Oberlin Conservatory Chorus; Member, A Cappella Choir.

EDUCATION

M.A. Renaissance Music History and Instrumentation, State University of New York, Syracuse, 1977.

B.A. Musical Performance and Direction, Oberlin Conservatory of Music, Oberlin, Ohio, 1975.

EMPLOYMENT HISTORY

1985-current: Director of Fundraising, Syracuse Community Arts Council, Syracuse, NY
Develop fundraising programs and efforts. Coordinate solicitation and disbursement of funds. Establish fundraising goals and policies for collecting contributions. Establish relationships with local, regional, and national organizations and coordinate events, support bases, and contacts.

1980-1985: Assistant Publicist, Syracuse Community Arts Council, Syracuse, NY
Wrote press releases, delivered presentations, and designed fliers and posters announcing competitions and events. Organized community events. Coordinated the 1984 Arts in the Park celebration in downtown Syracuse.

1975-1985: Taught voice, piano, and violin lessons on an individual basis. Instructed children and adults in basic music theory and technique.

REFERENCES PROVIDED UPON REQUEST

Evelyn Tickel • 4978 Broadway • Boulder, Colorado 80304 • 303-555-3892

Objective

A position as a high school science or environmental studies teacher

Education

University of Colorado, Boulder, CO, Teaching Certification, grades 1-12, 1992
Colorado State University, Fort Collins, CO, Bachelor of Science, Zoology, 1967

Professional Experience

Instructor, Boulder County Environmental Education Center, Boulder, CO
Instructed classes in zoology, environmental ecology, and plant and tree identification, using classroom and outdoor hands-on techniques. Supervised overnight trips for high school aged students. Developed and wrote booklet on endangered Colorado wildlife for use as textbook. *Volunteer, Part-time staff, 1990-present.*

Biological Assistant, University of Colorado Wildlife Department, Boulder, CO
Participated in capture, tagging, and relocation of bighorn sheep in Colorado, and in dietary studies of large ungulates. Assisted in research of black-capped chickadees: made sonogram recordings, maintained 75 birds. Assisted in research of endangered fish species in Western Colorado rivers: collected fish, identified species, collected data, performed literature search, and compiled and condensed information. *1989-1990.*

Consultant, Pokahu Ranch, Maui, Hawaii
Developed and wrote a conservation plan for the protection and restoration of the native ecosystem. Researched and evaluated the natural history, recovery plans, regulation, and recommendations of government officials. Performed species counts and determined the possibilities of rehabilitation of disturbed lands, eradication of pests, and reintroduction of endangered species. *April-June 1990.*

Scientific Technician, Washington State Department of Fisheries, Olympia, WA
Assisted in biological studies to assess the use of natural and artificial habitats by marine fish species for the purpose of developing criteria for habitat protection, mitigation, and enhancement. Collected and compiled data on salmonids for habitat protection and harvest management purposes, including species identification, length, weight, scale sampling, sex, mark sampling, tagging, and redd (salmon spawning "nests") identification. Identified marine micro-invertebrates for fish stomach analysis. Performed herring and smelt spawn surveys, plankton tows, beach seines, and eelgrass samples. Interviewed sport and commercial fishers. Prepared data summaries, charts, illustrations, and graphs. *Various departments, 1967-1989.*

References provided upon request

MARGARET HALVORSEN

154 Shoreline Drive
Chicago, IL 60611
(312) 555-1707 home • (312) 555-3602 office

OBJECTIVE

TECHNICAL WRITING AND EDITORIAL MANAGEMENT

HIGHLIGHTS OF QUALIFICATIONS

- Researched and wrote science biographies for technical reference books.
- Developed and wrote employee training manuals, catalogs, brochures, advertising copy, and press materials for retail businesses.
- Wrote and edited a broad range of grant proposals for technical and lay audiences.
- Developed, wrote, and designed public relations and fund-raising materials.
- Strong background in word processing, desktop publishing, and graphics software on Macintosh and IBM computer platforms.

WORK EXPERIENCE

Director, Corporate & Foundation Relations, University of Chicago Office of Development, Chicago, IL. 1985-present.

Grant Writer, Fund-Raising & Development Office, University of Chicago Press, Chicago, IL. 1980-85.

Promotions Assistant, University Book Stores, Inc., Austin, TX. 1975-80.

Program Manager and Events Coordinator, Pattersen's Books, Chicago, IL. 1970-75.

EDUCATION

Columbia University. B.A. with Distinction, Phi Beta Kappa, English with Creative Writing Emphasis. 1970.

Additional coursework included microbiology, chemistry, calculus, geology, statistics, and computer science.

WRITING PORTFOLIO AND REFERENCES AVAILABLE

RESUME

Pamela Miles
33 Hardesty Lane Apt 34
Tallahassee, FL 32303
904 555-9283

Objective:	A position as Art Teacher at the primary or secondary school level
Education:	Teacher's Certification for primary and secondary art instruction, 1992. B.S., Art (Humanities and Social Sciences), Florida State University, 1971.
Qualification Highlights:	• Certified to teach Art in the State of Florida. • Experienced with teaching grade school children arts and crafts projects at Children's Activity Center. • Knowledgeable of art media and techniques, including computer graphics. • Experienced at planning schedules, events, and programs.
Professional Work Experience:	Director of Development Communications 1980-present, Office of Development, Florida State University, Tallahassee. Plan and direct the public information program of the FSU Office of Development. Organize the design and production of organizational publications and plan the annual publications schedule. Gather information to write news releases and feature articles. Publications Coordinator 1977-1980, Searway/McKenna/Morris, Architects/Planners, Raleigh, NC. Wrote, edited, and submitted articles to professional/trade journal. Associate Editor, The Biological Scientist 1973-1977, American Association of Biological Scientists, Tallahassee, FL. Designed *The Biological Science Record,* a quarterly publication of the College of Biological Sciences. Designer, Display Advertising Department 1970-1973, *Florida Sun-Times,* Tallahassee. Designed advertisements, prepared layouts, created artwork and promotional ads, sold advertising; handled general administrative/record keeping duties; organized and conducted tours of the plant.
Relevant Activities	Member, Tallahassee Art Alliance, 1980-present. Volunteer, Children's Activity Center, 1985-present. Computer Graphic Art Workshop, Apple Computer, Inc., Tallahassee, FL (1 day). Desktop Design and Publishing Seminar by Robert Parks, Tallahassee, FL (7 days).

References provided on request

BRIAN WEBLEY •• 345 Coral View, Apt. 9B •• Coral Gables, Florida 33128 •• 305•555•7823

OBJECTIVE

Production Management Position with Process-Color Printing Firm

SUMMARY

23 years experience in all aspects of printing technology and production
Technical background in publishing, graphic arts, printing, and systems
15 years in printing department management
Developed innovative programs for cost-savings and increased productivity
Experienced mechanical engineer with thorough knowledge of printing equipment

CAREER EXPERIENCE

MANAGER OF GRAPHIC ARTS ENGINEERING   1978 to present
D.E.C. Printing Group, Southeastern Division, Miami, Florida

•• Specified and managed $175 million in lithography for twelve printers in the division.

•• Enhanced profitability as a result of involvement in procurement, planning, printing, and quality assurance programs, and the introduction of technological innovations.

•• Directed 80 professional and technical people in five departments at the central plant.

•• Worked closely with management in Quality Assurance/Target Management program, which increased efficiency by a margin of nearly 35 percent.

PRINTING OPERATIONS ENGINEER   1970 to 1978
Graphic Color, Subsidiary of D.E.C. Printing Group, Miami, Florida

•• Operated and maintained working conditions for seven Heidelberg six-color presses.

•• Designed work flow process that increased efficiency and press production by 20 percent.

•• Supervised crew of 20 press operators and 5 technicians.

•• Worked closely with stripping and camera departments to ensure highest quality press output.

TECHNICAL ENGINEER   1964 to 1969
Benberg-Lenz Manufacturing, Miami, Florida

•• Worked as engineer on production development team.

•• Assisted with design and testing of printing presses for color lithography.

EDUCATION

B.S. Mechanical Engineering, Arizona State University, 1964

References on request

Montreal, Quebec

Angelita Bergman
884 N.W. 12th Avenue
Fort Worth, Texas 76109
(214) 555-1985 (D)
(817) 555-9712 (E/W)

Summary of Qualifications
General management executive with 15 years experience in corporate sales, marketing, customer service, development, and distribution.

Experience

DaMark-Dolin America Corp.   1978 - 1993
  A $640 million Fortune 500 public corporation serving the cosmetics industry.

  EXECUTIVE VICE PRESIDENT   Dallas, Texas 1989 - 1993
  Catalog and Commercial Division. Directed sales, marketing, customer relations, and distribution for a two-plant, $180 million sales operation. Combined two acquired companies into the second-largest corporate division. Eliminated $325,000 in duplication costs. Designed national marketing strategy that produced a 15 percent sales increase. Generated 30 percent increase in new-business sales by expanding and upgrading product production. Increased profits by a margin of 23 percent in one year by enlarging client base and controlling prices. Improved quality control and productivity by reorganizing departments and centralizing support functions.

  CORPORATE OFFICER AND VICE PRESIDENT   Houston, Texas 1985 - 1989
  Corporate Management Division. Directed strategic acquisition, business development, marketing, and venture subsidiaries. Directed major capital expenditures, business plans, and incentive programs for twelve business units. Formulated corporate mission and established long range strategic plan, which led to supervision of major restructuring decisions. Completed several acquisitions and strategic divestitures that expanded the corporate profit margin approximately 18 percent.

  DIRECTOR OF CORPORATE DEVELOPMENT   Houston, Texas 1978 - 1985
  Corporate Management Division. Spearheaded four years of product design diversification, resulting in the corporation's first major market breakthrough in the pharmaceutical industry. Managed all business and venture development, including acquisitions, new technologies, start-ups, joint ventures, and leasing agreements.
  Directed development of a new manufacturing line of medicinal lotions through acquisition of Soltero, Inc. Improved plant productivity by 15 percent.

Early Career Positions   1970 - 1978
  Operations Management, WemCo Inc., Houston, Texas
  Design Module Leader, Patterson Corporation, Houston, Texas
  Project Team Leader, Patterson Corporation, Shreveport, Louisiana

Education

  Louisiana State University, M.S., Chemical Engineering & Business, 1978
  University of Montana, B.S., Mechanical Engineering, 1970

References available on request

KEVIN L. BAUER
3890 43rd AVE
ANN ARBOR, MICHIGAN 48106
313 • 555 • 3892

CAREER SUMMARY

General management executive with significant broad based experience in consumer, manufacturing, and publishing businesses. Technical background in publishing, graphic arts, printing, and systems. Proven leadership and expertise in:

- Sales
- Marketing
- Operations Management

- Strategic Planning
- Business Development & Acquisitions
- Financial Analysis

PROFESSIONAL EXPERIENCE

D.D. WILLIAMS CORPORATION, 1985-Current
A $1 billion Fortune 500 public corporation serving niche printing and graphics/video markets.
Executive Vice President, Santo Catalog and Commercial Group, Ann Arbor, Michigan, 1989-Current
- Directed sales, marketing, customer services, estimating, and distribution for a two-plant $125 million sales printing operation.
- Combined two acquired companies into the second largest corporate business group eliminating $250,000 in duplication.
- Designed a national, market-driven strategy which delivered a seventeen percent increase in sales.
- Generated new business sales of thirty percent in response to expanded and upgraded manufacturing equipment requirements.
- Increased profits twenty-eight percent through focus on prospecting and pricing control. Improved control and productivity by reorganizing sales assignments and centralizing sales support functions.

Corporate Officer and Vice President, Oshkosh, Wisconsin, 1985-1989
- Key member of Corporate Management (executive) Committee with broad strategic, acquisition, business development, and marketing responsibility and authority in a lean and highly autonomous corporate structure.
- Directed major capital expenditures, business plans, and incentives for twelve autonomous business units. Key board member for venture subsidiaries.
- Formulated corporate mission and market strategy which led to major restructuring decisions.
- Completed the purchase and transitionally directed the Peters Companies, adding five new subsidiaries and two new print markets and expanding sales by over $200 million.
- Accomplished other acquisitions and strategic divestitures, including the sale of the Flexible Packaging Group (two plants, $50 million sales) and the decision to divest the video group (five companies, $45 million sales).
- Established the long range strategy for the D.D. Williams Publications Groups (two plants, $43 million sales) and the strategic plan to create the D.D. Williams Pre-Press Group (three plants, $18 million sales) including the group management organization and startup of Color Response-Minnesota.
- Spearheaded a corporate identity campaign which emphasized D.D. Williams' national scope; developed a new corporate name which sparked investor and Wall Street interest.

GREETING CARDS, INC., 1968-1985
A $1.5 billion market leader in consumer and publishing products.
Director of Corporate Development, Kansas City, Missouri, 1981-1985
- Spearheaded four-year diversification program resulting in Greeting's first major acquisitions of Beel & Craig ($254 million sales) and SSN (educational, specialty, and consumer software publisher).
- Managed all business/venture development including acquisitions, new technologies, start-ups, joint ventures, and licensing agreements.
- Directed an electronics venture start-up and an acquired educational software subsidiary.

Manager of Graphic Arts Engineering, Kansas City, Missouri, 1977-1981
- Specified and managed $50 million of lithography purchased from six printers.
- Enhanced product profitability as a result of involvement in procurement, planning, manufacturing, quality assurance, and introduction of technological innovations.
- Directed ninety professional and technical personnel in four departments.

Operations Manager, Kansas City, Missouri, 1973-1976
- Generated productivity, schedule, and quality improvements involving sixty professional and technical personnel in five cities. Performed research for new products and business concepts.
- Improved productivity by fifteen percent, cut material waste, and reduced cycle time by fifty percent as supervisor of seventy-five technical and artistic personnel.

EARLY CAREER POSITIONS, 1968-1973

Manager of Graphic Arts Production Control
Design Module Leader-Corporate Schedule and Control System
High Potential Management assignments in field sales, treasury, and manufacturing supervision

EDUCATION

University of Massachusetts, Amherst, 1968, M.S., Industrial Engineering

University of Tennessee, Knoxville, 1966, B.S., Mechanical Engineering, Business minor

REFERENCES UPON REQUEST

JONATHAN B. OWENS   2245 RIVER ROAD
                                          NEWPORT, OR 97366
                                          503 555-2435

OBJECTIVE

After twenty years of active duty in the Coast Guard, I am seeking a management position in Program Development and Implementation which will utilize my extensive background in these areas.

EDUCATION

Master of Arts in Educational Administration, University of Oregon, Eugene, OR
Bachelor of Science in Human Relations and Organizational Behavior, U of O, Eugene, OR

EXPERIENCE

1989-present: Branch Chief for Emergency Medical Central Training Center, U.S. Coast Guard, Newport, OR
Responsibilities
Developed, designed, and implemented the curriculum for training Coast Guard personnel. Responsible for selecting and evaluating a staff of 30. Managed an annual budget of $200,000 for staff training and operations.
Contributions
Established new computer system to improve communications utilizing electronic mail. Developed and implemented new internal and external valuation programs to test new performance based curricula. Designed and implemented new instructor development plans which included continuing educational programs for personnel.

1987-1989: Operations Officer, U.S. Coast Guard, Ilwaco, WA
Responsibilities
Scheduled all ship movement activities. Supervised program for conducting boardings at sea to ensure compliance of commercial and recreational vessels to federal law. Supervised 20 personnel, including training and evaluation.
Contributions
Developed new unit training program by fostering a supportive educational environment.

1985-1987: Operations Officer, U.S. Coast Guard, Bethel, AK
Responsibilities
In charge of vessel traffic control for the safe passage of large crude oil carriers traveling in and out of Prince William Sound. Managed work schedules for both vessel traffic and communications watch standing personnel. Responsible for training, development, and performance evaluations for 15 personnel. Managed the maintenance of a remote microwave communications and vessel traffic radar system for all of Prince William Sound.
Contributions
Installed new radar tracking system which included upgrading remote power supply unit for one radar site. Improved personnel watch rotations to maximize time spent on the job as well as improve flexibility of time off. Implemented the hiring of civilian employees to replace Coast Guard personnel as permanent watch standers in the Vessel Traffic Center. Improved relations between Coast Guard and Maritime Industries.

JONATHAN B. OWENS, page 2

1983-1985: Administration Officer, U.S. Coast Guard Marine Safety Office, Ilwaco, WA
Responsibilities
In charge of personnel and supply administration for a 50-person unit. Direct supervisor of 7 personnel, including training and performance evaluations. Managed an annual budget of $350,000 for the maintenance and upkeep of an office building and a 29-unit housing complex.
Contributions
Centralized administrative personnel to take a team approach to handle all unit administrative matters. Eliminated unnecessary reports. Expedited the process of all administrative work by purchasing new computer hardware and software to increase efficiency.

1981-1983: Deck Maintenance Officer, U.S. Coast Guard, Ilwaco, WA
Responsibilities
Supervised personnel involved with all exterior maintenance of the ship, which included all deck machinery and small boats. Responsible for training and performance evaluations of 24 personnel.
Contributions
Improved group harmony by making the more unpleasant tasks an enjoyable experience by working as a team.

1980-1981: Assistant Branch Chief, U.S. Coast Guard Reserve Schools, San Diego, CA
Responsibilities
In charge of all activities involved with training Coast Guard Reserve personnel attending the training center. Supervised 30 personnel, including training and performance evaluations. Managed an annual budget of $250,000 for the operation of all reserve schools and facilities as well as a small-boat training unit.
Contributions
Implemented new training procedures for conducting reserve basic indoctrination course. Expanded small-boat handling course to include local active duty units. Provided budget and administrative input to small-boat training units.

1977-1980: Instructor, Leadership School, U.S. Coast Guard, San Diego, CA
Responsibilities
Involved with developing, designing, and implementing curriculum for newly established leadership and management program for Coast Guard personnel.
Contributions
Developed two-week curriculum for the school from the latest leadership and management practices. Participated in design, development, and testing of the new performance evaluation system currently used by the Coast Guard.

1973-1977: Joined U.S. Coast Guard, Newport, OR
Responsibilities
Front line employee with no supervising responsibilities.

OTHER INTERESTS
Board of Directors, Newport Youth Soccer League
Coach, Newport Community Youth Basketball Leagues

REFERENCES AVAILABLE UPON REQUEST

Marcia Penas Smith

555 Alexandria Street
Apt. 35
Washington, D.C., 20013
(202) 555-0988

OBJECTIVE

A position as translator for a federal or state agency

LANGUAGES

Fluent in written and spoken Spanish, Portuguese, and French

EDUCATION

M.A. Spanish and Portuguese, 1992, Middlebury College, Middlebury, VT
B.A. French and Psychology, 1970, Arizona State University, Tempe, AZ
Foreign Study program in Oaxaca, Mexico, 1969-1970, Arizona State University

WORK EXPERIENCE

English teacher, English Department, Madrid University, Spain. 1988-1990.
Taught reading and conversation to undergraduates and teachers of non-English majors. Developed curriculum for and taught elective reading course on North American short stories. Taught beginning conversation to small group of primary school students. Informally advised Spanish students on living and studying in the U.S.

Assistant to Director, Office of International Education, Arizona State System of Higher Education, Arizona State University. 1980-1988.
Developed and administered Latin American summer exchange program for high school students. Assisted with foreign student and foreign study orientation programs. Coordinated visits of international guests. Assisted in administration of foreign study programs.

Office Assistant, Office of International Programs and Summer Session, Arizona State University. 1972-1980.
Assisted in administration of overseas programs. Assisted with information meetings and pre-departure orientations. Gave general advising to students interested in study and work abroad. Handled Summer Session and special program registrations. Responsible for general secretarial-receptionist duties.

Co-facilitator, Intercultural Communication Workshop, ASU. 1971-1972.
Facilitated groups of American and foreign students through ten-week workshops designed to develop participants' cross-cultural communication skills. Lead discussions and supervised activities which provided experiential learning. Planned sessions with other facilitators and workshop leaders.

REFERENCES AVAILABLE UPON REQUEST

Anna Robinson
P.O. Box 389
Cheyenne, Wyoming 82001
307-555-2983

OBJECTIVE   To teach at the secondary school level

EDUCATION
- M.Ed. and Certification, University of Colorado, Greeley, 1992
- B.A., Elementary Education, University of Michigan, Ann Arbor, 1968
- Wyoming Real Estate Broker's License, Rocky Mountain School of Real Estate, Cheyenne, WY, 1979
- Wyoming Real Estate Sales License, Professional Institute of Real Estate, Laramie, WY, 1975

RELEVANT EXPERIENCE

Reading and Writing Tutor and Student Teacher, Greeley School District, Greeley, CO, 1991-1992

Advisor, Entrepreneurial Youth, Inc., Cheyenne, WY, 1980-present

Classroom Teacher, Tyler School District, Tyler, MI, 1968-1975
Taught grades 1 through 7, specialized in Language Arts.

PROFESSIONAL EXPERIENCE

Designated Broker, Sales and Marketing Director, Courtmore Homes, Inc., Cheyenne, WY, 1979-1990
- Responsibilities included: development of purchase contract package; contract approval; design of brochures, advertising, model home complexes; development of product line, floor plans, and elevations; consultation concerning land acquisition and development; hiring, supervision, and support of subdivision sales staff and decorating personnel.

Sales Representative, Homeland, Inc., Cheyenne, WY, 1975-1979
- Responsibilities included: subdivision sales, contract writing, buyer relations and closings, and sales office / model complex management

REFERENCES AVAILABLE ON REQUEST

PETER J. LUCERO
3876 Maple Street
Topeka, KS 66603
913 555-9835

CAREER OBJECTIVE

A career position in international relations or operations with a multinational corporation or major organization.

SUMMARY OF SKILLS

- Multi-lingual administrator, educator, lecturer in Spanish, German, French, and English.
- Associate pastor and director of a Chicago inner-city parish complex, an upwardly mobile Catholic community in Kansas, and a popular parish in Frankfurt, Germany.
- Regional consultant to the New York electronic media.
- Member, Board of Directors, for a non-profit housing development corporation.
- Director of professional, paraprofessional, and volunteer staffs in four countries.
- Coordinator of private- and government-sponsored relief activities for Central American refugees.
- Chaplain and advisor to international business and diplomatic communities.
- Liaison between church authorities, civic officials, and professional groups in the greater Frankfurt metropolitan area.
- Academic advisor to graduate students on University of Kansas campus.

CAREER HISTORY

Assistant Administrator, Associate Pastor, St. Mary's Church, Topeka, KS, 1991-1992.
- As member of religious education staff, recruited, trained, and evaluated performance of 100 volunteer teaching/clerical support personnel.
- Created and conducted adult seminar groups, stressing contemporary moral and ethical problems.

Assistant Administrator, Catholic Archdiocese, Frankfurt, Germany, 1984-1990.
- Initiated German-American lecture series on socio-political, moral, and religious themes.
- Regularly presided at multi-lingual liturgical functions in international congregations.
- Provided pastoral counseling, in three languages, to English, French, and German speaking communities in Frankfurt.
- Liaison between church officials and civic, business, and diplomatic leaders.
- Supervised educational programs for parish residents and their children.

Member, Administrative & Counseling Staff, Graduate Student, Jesuit College of Theology, Boston, MA, 1981-1984.
- Served as academic advisor and pastoral counselor to resident graduate students while pursuing doctoral degree.
- Assisted in developing efficient administrative structures, challenging curricula, relevant practica, and appropriate criteria for the selection and training of those destined for ministry.

Assistant Administrator, Missionary Priest, Tegucigalpa, Honduras, January 1980-July 1981.
- Served all levels of local, national, and international society in Honduras, from campesinos and refugees to professional and business classes and diplomatic personnel.
- Assisted in the pastoral and material care of these groups, focusing on the plight of displaced persons, the educational and health-care needs of indigenous populations, and the training and development of their civic, political, and religious leaders.
- Acted as liaison between these groups and international relief agencies.

LUCERO, page 2

Assistant Administrator, Our Lady of Hope Church, Chicago, IL, 1978-1980.
- Reorganized, funded, and supervised education programs for more than 1,000 children and adults in this inner-city, bilingual community.
- Revised curricula and trained professional, paraprofessional, and volunteer support staffs.
- Acted as conduit for municipal public assistance grants and federal and state agency funds for advocacy and outreach programs.
- Appointed member, Board of Directors of "Casa Nueva Housing Corporation" (a nonprofit, regional corporation with advocacy, outreach, and educational functions) and "Adopt a Building" (a nonprofit organization engaged in rehabilitation of abandoned buildings for lower-middle income).
- Applied for and received Federal (HUD) grant of $10 million for 145 family units.
- Served as Consultant on Community Affairs to Vice President, Creative Services, WALL-Radio, functioning as liaison between this major regional station and the needs, aspirations, and programs of local communities.

Chaplain of St. Rose's Home, Chicago, IL, 1978-1980.
Served concurrently with the latter position, as Chaplain at this home for terminally ill cancer patients:
- Attended to the spiritual, psychological, and counseling needs of patients and their families.
- Recruited, trained, and monitored performance of more than 100 volunteers.
- Performed traditional functions of active clergyman in major urban hospital environment.

EDUCATION

St. Peter College, Newport, RI, B.A. Cum Laude, Sociology/Philosophy
Harvard Divinity School, Cambridge, MA, M.Div.
Jesuit College of Theology, Boston, MA, S.T.L. (advanced Master of Arts), Magna Cum Laude.
Catholic Institute of Germany, Frankfurt, Germany, S.T.D./ Ph.D. Candidate.

PROFESSIONAL ASSOCIATIONS / CIVIC-VOLUNTEER ORGANIZATIONS

Member, **Ecumenical Council,** Topeka, KS, 1991-1992.
Member, **Community Frankfurt** (business / residential group promoting area development), Frankfurt, Germany, 1988-1990.
Member, **WSAC** (West Side Area Conference), Chicago, 1978-1980.
Member, Board of Directors, **"Casa Nueva Housing Corporation"** (part of the Neighborhood Housing Advocacy, Advisory Administrative Group), Chicago, 1978-1980.
Member, Board of Directors, **Adopt a Building,** Chicago, 1978-1980.
Consultant in community affairs to V.P., **Creative Services WALL-Radio**, Chicago, 1978-1980.
Counselor, **St Peter's Inn**, Detoxification and Rehabilitation Center, Piedmont, IL, 1975-1978.
Chaplain's Assistant / Counselor, **Mildred State Hospital,** Parker, IL; 1975-1976.
Volunteer, **Catholic Worker Movement**, Chicago, summers, 1972-1973.
Volunteer Extern, **Jewish Memorial Hospital & Boston City Hospital**, Boston, MA, 1970-1971.

REFERENCES AVAILABLE

JoAnna Weber

P.O. Box 34
Phoenix, Arizona 85034
602-555-0938

Objective: Office manager for travel agency, with opportunity to train in tour management.

Experience

Office Manager, Saxton Microflox, Phoenix, Arizona
1991 to present

Responsible for all central support operations, bookkeeping staff, and office planning and administration. Maintain payroll records, process federal and state tax reports. Handle cost accounting and general ledger reports. Direct hiring and supervision of office staff. Respond to requests from engineering and executive departments for special project support.

Travel Coordinator, Saxton Microflox, Phoenix, Arizona
1989 to 1991

Responsible for coordinating all travel arrangements for engineers and executives traveling nationally and internationally. Processed payments and payment vouchers. Maintained data file of travel resources.

Secretary, West Phoenix School District, Phoenix, Arizona
1980 to 1989

Provided secretarial support to principal and faculty. Extensive public relations contact with students, parents, faculty, and general public. Responsible for bookkeeping and supply inventory. Supervised central office staff.

Secretary, JKN Architects, Salt Lake City, Utah
1972 to 1980

Typed proposals and specifications lists. Responsible for payroll and general bookkeeping. High level of public contact with contractors, clients, and general public.

Accounting and Sales, Jered's Sporting Goods Store, Salt Lake City, Utah
1968 to 1972

Held responsibility for accounts payable. Handled sales and balanced receipts. Prepared deposits. Provided switchboard relief.

Production Typist, Smithfield Insurance Company, Salt Lake City, Utah
1967 to 1968

Education

A.A. Degree, Office Systems, Salt Lake Business College, Salt Lake City, Utah
1972

References will be provided on request.

Joseph Monroe   3892 Beverly Road
                                                Springfield, MA 01101
                                                    413 555-3982

Objective: A position in Marketing and Sales Management of a radio station which would utilize my skills as a corporate executive and my extensive experience in sales management in the manufacturing field.

Education:

M.B.A., University of Massachusetts, Amherst, 1980
B.A., Business Administration, Communications and Radio, Ohio University, Athens, 1964

Professional Experience:

As **Vice President of Sales & Marketing**, Amco Corporation, 1980-present:
- Develop marketing strategies to support customer and operator needs.
- Coordinate between administrative, sales, and operations branches to provide manufacturing with standards and goals.
- Oversee relations with 50 top customers, representing more than $250 million in annual revenue.
- Supervise 20 sales staff and coordinate with Operations and Administration departments.
- Negotiated product and service changes with U.S. Postal Service, maintaining cost standard for a savings of $1 million over 5 years.
- Improved productivity by 45 percent in 2-year period with design and implementation of employee participatory program.
- Supervised a marketing and promotion effort that saw sales improve 15 percent in the first quarter, 25 percent in the second quarter after implementation.

As **Sales and Marketing Manager**, Amco Corporation, 1965-1979:
- Supervised all sales people.
- Negotiated contracts with 20 top customers.
- Managed all customer fulfillment and complaints.
- Responsible for development and marketing of product changes and new services.
- Negotiated new and renewed contracts with 20 customers, representing an annual revenue of $100 million.
- Established a standard sales training program in-house, which improved efficiency and consistency in customer relations.

As **Station Manager**, WIML Radio, Ohio University, 1963-1965:
- Managed budgets and staffing schedules.
- Supervised fundraising and programming, scheduling and publicity for radio station.

As **Programming Director**, WIML Radio, Ohio University, 1962-1963:
- Planned, reviewed, and revised all programming for station.
- Scheduled all on-air personnel.
- Hosted a classical and interview program.

Memberships:

Board member, Corporation for Public Radio, Massachusetts.
Supporting member, Springfield Symphony.
Member, Marketing Association of America.

Professional and personal references furnished on request.

Juanita Rodriguez-Sutton
330 Hollywood Boulevard
Los Angeles, California 90063
(213) 555-2475 days
(213) 555-0248 message

Career Objective: Seeking position as Advertising Director for a large west coast agency.

Achievements

- Handled distribution, retail marketing, advertising, and mail order marketing for weekly news magazine with more than 2 million circulation.
- Wrote advertising copy and made sales presentations to clients and account executives.
- Handled advertising accounts worth in excess of $1.5 million as Marketing and Promotions Director for FM radio station.
- Obtained knowledge of domestic and overseas regulations for trademarks.
- Assisted marketing director with radio and television promotion and retail marketing.
- Coordinated radio and print interview opportunities for visiting artists and writers.
- Developed and implemented print and broadcast advertising campaign for major retail chain.
- Directed research department for market data and sales reports.

Work History

LA Productions Weekly, Los Angeles, CA
- Marketing Director, 9/88 to present
- Public Relations/Marketing Assistant, 6/82 to 7/88

KBOQ Radio, Venice, CA
- Marketing and Promotions Director, 5/77 to 6/80
- Promotions Assistant, 3/76 to 5/77

Macy's, San Francisco, CA
- Marketing Department, 6/72 to 3/76.

Education

University of California, Los Angeles
- Post-baccalaureate study in Advertising and Marketing, 9/80 to 6/82
- Bachelor of Science in Journalism/Public Relations, 6/72

References upon request

JEAN K. SCHUMANN
389 SW 13th AVENUE
OLYMPIA, WA 97301
206 555-3982

CAREER OBJECTIVE

To obtain a position as Scientific Technician for the Washington Department of Fisheries or the U.S. Department of Natural Resources.

SUMMARY OF EXPERIENCE

- Collected biological data as Biological Aide at Washington Coastal Aquarium.
- Participated in field study emphasizing terrestrial vegetation, geological features, and marine organisms, and maintained field journal of activities, including transect and plot studies.
- Participated in compiling environmental report for county sub-area plan, producing vegetation map, writing and editing sections of report, and presenting group results to planning committee.
- Maintained records of shipments, collected and prepared ore samples for chemical analysis, and assisted in surveying for Taber Shipments, Inc.
- Developed and implemented Marine Biology (Intertidal Organisms and Rocky and Cobbled Shore Habitat) and Cedar and Salmon Natural and Cultural History Programs for use at girl scout camps.
- Assisted in supervising and training staff, planning programs, and evaluating performance and programs.
- Taught and led nature activities for children and adults in marine and terrestrial biology, intertidal habitats and organisms, forest ecosystems and habitats, botany, zoology, and meteorology.
- Supervised trip planning and taught skills in equipment use, map reading, fire making, shelter building, and minimum-impact camping.

WORK HISTORY

Community Resource Staff, Campus Recreation Center, Deschutes University, Olympia, WA, *1985-present.*
Assistant Director, Program Planner, Rainier Girl Scout Council, Tacoma, WA, *1980-1985.*
Program Development Intern, Rainier Girl Scout Council, Tacoma, WA, *1979.*
Biological Aide, Washington Coast Aquarium, Long Beach, WA, *Summers, 1975-1979.*
Biological Assistant, Taber Shipments, Inc., Spokane, WA, *1974.*

EDUCATION

Deschutes University, Olympia, WA
1979, Bachelor of Arts, Environmental Education and Bachelor of Science, Biology

REFERENCES AVAILABLE ON REQUEST

J. WILLIAM CLARK
4437 WHITE OAKS DRIVE
URBANA, IL 61801
(309) 555-2847 (VOICE)
(309) 555-3345 (FAX)

OBJECTIVE
An executive position in an organization involved with public policy and finance.

PROFESSIONAL EXPERIENCE

Lecturer, Management and Public Administration————————————
Graduate Center, University of Illinois, Urbana-Champaign, 1979 to 1993
    Taught organizational management courses for the College of Business. Topics
    included: Managing Organizations (process of organizing, planning, and
    controlling), Organizational Behavior (leadership, internal politics, and group
    dynamics), The Global Business Environment (domestic and international political,
    economic, and social issues that affect complex organizations), and Public Policy
    Administration (development, structure, and implementation of public policy).

Executive Consultant, Social Policy and Study Center————————————
George Washington University, Washington, D.C., 1973 to 1979
    Developed and taught seminars on organizational management and global economic
    issues in business for officials from the governments of fourteen countries.
    Coordinated the development of an Equal Employment Opportunity Plan for a
    major public policy research organization. Represented senior management with the
    government auditing agency requiring the affirmative action plan. Other principal
    clients included the Economic Policy Research Institute, the American Center for the
    Study of Behavior, and W.W. Group International, an organization that monitors
    and analyzes public policy issues throughout the world.

Assistant Executive Director, National School Boards Association————————————
Washington, D.C., and Chicago, Illinois, 1968 to 1973
    Planned, organized, developed, and coordinated programs and activities for the
    national network of school district trustees from the nation's urban centers.
    Consulted with the Director of the President's Commission on School Finance, the
    Executive Director of the Education Commission of the States, and the National
    Advisory Committee on Career Education.

Program Associate, National Public Schools Support Association————————————
Washington, D.C., 1965 to 1968
    Held full financial accountability for budgeting, planning, controlling, and
    personnel management. Provided consulting services to school districts and support
    organizations nationally.

Previous employment includes three years as a public school teacher in Illinois and four
    years active duty as an officer in the U.S. Navy.

EDUCATION

Ph.D. Politics and Public Policy Administration
George Washington University, 1972

M.B.A. Finance and Administration
Purdue University, 1965

B.A. Business and Economics (NROTC)
Purdue University, 1960

MEMBERSHIPS

National Field Task Force for the Improvement and Reform of American Education, U.S.
    Office of Education
Retired Naval Reserve Officers Association

REFERENCES ON REQUEST

KARL LI

290 SUMMIT DRIVE
PORTLAND, OR 97208
503 555-0709

OBJECTIVE: A management position in sales or promotion for a quality manufacturing corporation

PROFESSIONAL EXPERIENCE

EXECUTIVE DIRECTOR (April 1990-present) Willamette Valley Health Care Foundation, Portland, Oregon.

Provide direction for the Foundation. Responsibilities include strategic planning, fund-raising, program development, volunteer development, and grant writing. Produce, sponsor, and coordinate the annual festival, Healthfest. Conduct a needs assessment for Willamette Valley as a measure of program effectiveness. Plan annual community fund-raising campaign and membership campaign. Serve as Vice President of Oregon Non-Profits Association. On Portland Regional Hospital Finance Committee; Willamette Community Health Council, Oregon.

REGIONAL DIRECTOR (1985-April 1990) The Children's Foundation, Chicago, Illinois.

Provided strategic management and hands-on assistance to 11 chapters, in 9 states. Offered expertise in fund-raising, finance, volunteer development, staff training, and programs. With chapter directors, established goals and objectives for chapter performance. Evaluated achievements against goals. Hired, trained, and supervised chapter directors and regional offices staff. Directed 115 employees. Planned and conducted two training meetings per year for chapter directors and other key staff/volunteers. Acted as a resource to other regional directors on the subject of budgets, finance, and quantitative analysis. Served on the board of The National Children's Foundation, 1987-1990. Established a volunteer, region-wide data base consisting of executive committee members and key volunteer leadership in 1987, with annual updates.

EXECUTIVE DIRECTOR (1983-1985) The Children's Foundation, Midwest Region, Des Moines, Iowa.

Responsible for the administration of the local chapter, including fundraising and program development. The door-to-door campaign led the nation in per capita revenue, the highest per capita to date, anywhere in the nation. Our largest sponsor-based event, Lifewalk, was expanded to the point where every community of 5,000+ held the event. Improved collection procedures and enhanced revenue. Influenced a reversal of Des Moines School Board policy to allow The Children's Foundation access to schools for fund-raising.

SPECIAL EVENTS CONSULTANT (1980-1983) Iowa Heart Association, Des Moines.

Created two major fund-raising events: bike treks and backpacking treks. Developed volunteer and corporate resources for special event fund-raising in an agency heavily dependent on mail income.

KARL LI ADVERTISING AND PUBLIC RELATIONS (1979-1980), Des Moines.

Provided advertising and public relations services to a variety of clients, both profit and non-profit. Specialized in radio production/advertising.

KARL LI, p. 2

DEVELOPMENT DIRECTOR (1976-1978) Heart Research Institute, Chicago, Illinois.

Wrote and obtained grants from foundations for equipment and program support. Developed promotional and public relations activities designed to make the public aware of HRI's services. Facilitated enrollment of patients into HRI's programs. Helped HRI expand to new markets.

FIELD REPRESENTATIVE (1973-1976) The Children's Foundation, Chicago, Illinois.

Primary responsibility was volunteer recruitment and training in 16 volunteer chapters and five partially-staffed chapters in western Washington. Dramatically increased the revenue of these chapters nearly 50% in three years.

ACCOUNT EXECUTIVE (1972-1973) KUMO Radio, Chicago, Illinois.

Serviced and sold accounts. Wrote copy. Assisted in production. Director for Mutual Radio, Midwest. Provided live feed and delayed commercials for Central time slots.

EDUCATION

Master of Public Administration (MPA), University of Chicago, 1978.
Bachelor of Arts, Communications (BA), University of Chicago, 1972.

REFERENCES AVAILABLE ON REQUEST

LUCINA ALVAREZ
1283 Bramble Drive
Austin, TX 78710
(512) 555-1707 home • (512) 555-3602 office

OBJECTIVE

To obtain a position as senior technical editor for a large corporation

EDUCATION

Columbia University. M.A., English. GPA, 3.91. 1987.

Columbia University. B.A. with Distinction, Phi Beta Kappa,
English with Creative Writing Emphasis. 1970.

Additional coursework included chemistry, calculus, geology,
statistics, and computer science.

EXPERIENCE

1985-
present

Proposal Writer, Corporate & Foundation Relations,
University of Texas Office of Development, Austin, TX. Assist
administrators and faculty in writing and editing a broad range
of grant proposals for technical and lay audiences. Develop,
write, and design public relations and fund-raising materials for
the University's maximum priority projects. Review annual
reports and other corporate publications to identify major
donor prospects. Conduct quarterly seminars for staff and
faculty on proposal writing. Supervise student assistant.
During first year was involved in generating gifts to the
University totaling over $3.1 million.

1988-
present

Board of Directors, Fund-Raising Chair, Wild Rose Press,
Austin, TX. Hold volunteer administrative and fund-raising
responsibilities for small non-profit literary press. Write and edit
grant proposals to government agencies and private
foundations.

1980-
present

Freelance Writer, Graphic Designer, and Photographer,
Austin, TX. Services include color and black-and-white
photography, desktop publishing, and writing and editing
newsletters, catalogs, advertisements, feature articles, and
public relations materials. Recent project involved researching
and writing science biographies for technical reference book.

1975-
1985

Promotions Assistant, University Book Stores, Inc., Austin,
TX. Responsible for writing, designing, and producing store
brochures, flyers, signs, and advertisements. Required
extensive knowledge of desktop publishing, graphics, and
production methods.

1970-
1974
    Program Manager and Events Coordinator, Drake's Books & Magazines, New York, NY. Responsible for public relations and all aspects of weekly reading series at NYC's third largest independent bookseller. Designed and wrote all advertising copy, press releases, catalogs, brochures, and employee training manuals. Scheduled author appearances and hosted and introduced authors at events with audiences ranging from 50 to 400. Authors included Pulitzer Prize-winners Taylor Branch and Tracy Kidder and National Book Award-winner Stephen Jay Gould. Supervised a staff of two.

OTHER SKILLS

Expertise in WordPerfect and many other MS/DOS and Macintosh word processing, desktop publishing, and graphics programs.

RECENT PUBLICATIONS

6/91   "William Marcus," Barker's Survey of American Literature, Austin Press, Austin, TX.

2/91   "John Hope," The Nobel Prize Winners: Physiology and Medicine, Austin Press, Austin, TX.

2/91   "Miles Horne," The Nobel Prize Winners: Physiology and Medicine, Austin Press, Austin, TX.

COMPLETED MANUSCRIPTS

3/92   "On the Road with Peter Fabre," for American Artist Journal.

12/91   Understanding Media, with Lyle Roberts, Sherry Huber, and Alice Barker.

MEMBERSHIPS

Phi Beta Kappa, Toastmasters International, Council for the Advancement and Support of Education, and National Society of Fund-Raising Executives.

CURRENT REFERENCES & WRITING SAMPLES

Available upon request.

TAMARA MESERVEY
389 Southwest Fifteenth Avenue
Philadelphia, Pennsylvania 19104
(215) 555-2899

GOAL: A production management position in advertising on a large-circulation newspaper.

QUALIFICATIONS

- Experienced in all aspects of printing and pre-press processing equipment.
- Marketing, advertising, sales, graphic production.
- Records management, including accounts payable/receivable, payroll, inventory control, and tax reporting.
- Purchase of supplies to assure adequate inventories.
- Day-to-day management responsibilities, including scheduling, assigning activities, training, and program assessments.
- Experienced with computerized typesetting and pre-press graphic production.
- Public relations skills, including reception, sales, collections, and purchasing.
- Time management proficiency, promoting timely completion of projects and meeting deadlines.

EDUCATION

Community College of Philadelphia, Pennsylvania. 1991-present.
Business management courses with emphasis in retailing, advertising, marketing, accounting, and human relations.

Philadelphia College of Art, Pennsylvania. 1975-1977.
Associate of Arts Degree, Process Camera and Stripping.

EXPERIENCE

Management Assistant. Regional School of Ballet, Philadelphia. 1991-1992.
Duties: Learned and implemented managerial skills in daily management of dance school. Arranged advertising through local media sources. Planned development and marketing and advertising strategies. Completed billing reports, payroll records, compiled accounts payable and receivable information. Collected unpaid balances. Ordered and maintained inventories. Supervised staff and scheduled work hours.

Camera Operator/Printer. Sir Speedy Printing, Philadelphia. 1982-1991.
Duties: Operated variety of camera and bindery equipment, including printer and plate maker. Assisted customers, completed sales transactions and reports, prepared advertising for local media and yellow pages. Began system of tracking advertising results to better determine advertising cost-effectiveness.

Printer. In and Out Printing, Philadelphia. 1977-1982.
Duties: Operated printing machine and darkroom equipment. Coordinated incoming work assignments. Performed paste-up, plate making, and bindery duties. Trained newly assigned employees. Composed, printed, and generated monthly newsletter. Carried out projects as assigned.

REFERENCES AVAILABLE

Theresa Miller
33528 Santa Monica Boulevard
Los Angeles, California 90088
(213) 555-8842 (days)
(213) 555-3331 (eves)

Career Objective

Traffic manager for an advertising agency or corporate advertising department.

Work Experience

Connections Magazine, Hollywood, California
Production Manager, 1988 to present

Oversee all aspects of production and printing for a national publication. Involved in extensive client and advertising agency contact. Organize all art, mechanicals, and final films with stripping department. Coordinate with editorial and advertising department heads for positioning of advertising. Work with graphic designers on production specifications and proofing. Handle in-depth contact with other media and service vendors. Produce copy and mechanicals for advertisements.

L.A. Arts Weekly, Los Angeles, California
Advertising Manager, 1980 - 1988

Directed advertising sales for 45-page arts section of *L.A. Times.* Developed sales strategies, assigned territories to sales staff, conducted weekly sales report meetings, tracked sales and billing. Coordinated advertising design and production with graphic design staff. Directed preparation of mock-up ads for sales presentations to encourage regular, increased ad sales for target clients. Developed special ad pages for arts organizations and directed sales efforts.

Havener's, Burbank, California
Assistant to Promotion Director, 1974 - 1980

Conducted all in-store promotions and coordinated special events for large department store. Placed advertising and publicity notices in local media. Prepared advertising copy and design mock-ups for promotional ads. Wrote text for radio and television spot announcements. Consulted on grand opening of Hollywood store. Provided customer assistance.

Education

University of California, Los Angeles
B.S. in Advertising and Marketing, 1974

Honors: Cum Laude, 1974; Dean's List, 1972 - 1974; Wilma Morrison Scholarship, 1971 - 1974; National Association of Student Yearbooks, Advertising Sales Award, 1974, Best Advertising Design, 1974.

References provided upon request

ALTHEA BESSEY
4893 ARLINGTON DRIVE
INDIANAPOLIS, INDIANA 46201
(317) 555-9889

OBJECTIVE

A position in Marketing in a strongly customer-oriented, multi-national organization.

PROFESSIONAL EXPERIENCE

Research Scientist, International Feminine Care, Beverly Jones Corporation,
Indianapolis, 1989-present
- Evaluate, recommend, and develop product changes to meet performance
  expectations of a new feminine care product for three international regions of this
  Fortune 500, multi-national, consumer products company manufacturing such
  brand products as Bouncies and Comforts.
- Establish quantitative measures for subjective functional performance evaluations
  and product comparisons.
- Implement consistent market research plans for performance comparisons between
  regions.
- Work closely with international marketing research department in suggesting and
  implementing improvements to consumer market research questionnaires.
- Design product development plans for market research efforts.
- Obtain medical clearances, coordinate materials, prepare product samples, and
  schedule equipment and testing.
- Work with U.S. product development group to integrate U.S. and international
  program support.
- Provide engineering with product information for equipment designs.
- Participate in regional project update meetings in the U.S., Asia, Latin America, and
  Europe.
- Provide support to process trials in Mexico and Taiwan.
- Prepare reports on product functional tests.
- Participate on Product Development Seminar Committee to define format for
  company-wide seminar.

Scientist II, Scientist I, Senior Research Technician, Beverly Jones Corporation,
Indianapolis, 1979-1989
- Accountable for all aspects of product development for industrial wipers and
  washroom hand towels.
- Successfully developed new washroom hand towel product that out-performed
  market leader and returned twice the initial sales projections.
- Developed new market research techniques to define consumer language in
  describing products; translated and interpreted terminology for quantitative
  measures.
- Developed and validated mathematical model for determining user preference from
  physical test data.
- Developed several line extension products and implemented cost savings
  technologies for existing products.

- Member of multi-functional business team; assisted in defining market needs, designing products to meet cost requirements, verifying advertising claims, providing technical sales support, and implementing product roll-outs.
- Managed project budgets and established project objectives.
- Analyzed and resolved customer complaints regarding product performance; conducted one-on-one customer interviews and site visits.
- Provided process and product support for start-up of a new converting mill.
- Advised manufacturing personnel in converting operations to ensure product quality and specifications; assisted in trouble-shooting efforts.
- Wrote product specifications for manufacturing guidelines and worked with Quality Assurance for test methods and quality procedures.
- Consulted with packaging specialists to define packaging specifications.
- Initiated Quality House Directive (QHD) for service and industrial products; served on safety and Total Quality Management (TQM) committees.
- Co-chaired session for company-wide Product Development seminar; chaired committee to define product development in Service and Industrial Sector.
- Coached and mentored technicians through career development process.

Quality Assurance Superintendent, Techmill, Inc., Youngstown, OH, 1973-1979
- Organized and managed fifteen-person quality department for a new non-woven cloth manufacturing plant.
- Implemented corporate quality programs.
- Trained personnel and implemented statistical process control systems throughout the plant.
- Wrote and implemented a GMP manual for Class III medical device.

EDUCATION

M.B.A., Kennesaw State College, Kennesaw, GA, 1992.

B.S., Mathematics/Engineering, University of Minnesota, Crookston, MN, 1972.

REFERENCES AVAILABLE UPON REQUEST

GAVIN MCCLOUD   P.O. BOX 12, ST. PAUL, MN 53402 / 612-555-0932

Objective

A position as a high school science teacher

Education

University of Minnesota, Twin Cities, Minneapolis, MN, 1992, Master of Education

University of Vermont, Burlington, VT, 1966, Bachelor of Science

Professional Certification

Minnesota: Elementary, 1-6
             Middle and High School, 7-12

Related Skills and Experience

Taught classes in stream ecology, outdoor survival, backpacking, and trip planning. Supervised overnight trips for primary and secondary school students. Assisted in developing programs and designing courses aimed at integrating science education with outdoor activities.

Assisted in research on stream ecology and effects of pollutants: collected samples and other data, performed literature searches, and compiled and condensed information.

Prepared data summaries, charts, illustrations, and graphs; wrote summary reports; evaluated methods, procedures, and results of stream ecology studies.

Assisted in biological studies to assess natural and artificial habitats by woodland species for developing habitat protection, mitigation, and enhancement criteria.

Collected data on weasel population for habitat protection purposes.

Participated in capture, tagging, and monitoring of small mammals.

Employment History

Instructor, Minnesota Outdoor Center, St. Paul, MN. *Part-time staff, 1988-present.*

Biological Assistant, University of Minnesota Wildlife Department, Minneapolis, MN. *1989-1990.*

Biological Assistant, State of Minnesota Department of Wildlife, St. Paul, MN. *Various departments, 1967-1989.*

References provided upon request

Paula R. Roper
38402 Butte Lane
Fargo, North Dakota 58502
(701) 555-2908

PROFESSIONAL OBJECTIVE

A position as Customer Service Representative in a retail or service environment.

SKILLS HIGHLIGHTS

* Skilled at assisting clients, customers, and the public.
* Work well independently and as a team member.
* Work with thoroughness and attention to detail.
* High quality work in WordPerfect 5.0 and Lotus 1-2-3.
* Experienced with office organizational techniques.

EMPLOYMENT HISTORY

Administrative Assistant, City of Fargo, Fargo Fire Department, 1989-present.
Performed receptionist duties, answering inquiries and complaints. High volume of word processing and data entry of budget documents. Data entry and record keeping of Fire Incidents and Training Records. Process purchase orders. Team member of FireMed ambulance subscription program.

Municipal Court Clerk, City of Fargo, 1980-1989.
Completed record keeping for Court. Initiated Court correspondence, prepared Court docket. Compiled statistical reports. Prepared and submitted Court budget.

Administrative Assistant, Nuclear Engineering Department, North Dakota State University, Fargo, 1976-1980.
Interacted with public, student body, and potential clients of research teams as main receptionist for department. Maintained undergraduate student records. Compiled statistical reports. Completed typing of technical manuscripts, scientific reports, and correspondence.

Administrative Assistant for Mortgage Services, David A. Gilbert Co., Jamestown, North Dakota, 1972-1976.
Interacted with clients—set up appointments, made referrals, and handled all inquiries and complaints. Typed legal documents, including mortgages, deeds, closing statements, and escrow instructions. Drafted and typed correspondence and proposal packages. Organized and maintained extensive case and resource files.

EDUCATION

University of Oregon, Eugene, Oregon. 1972, B.A., Liberal Arts and Letters.
Mt. Angel College, Mt. Angel, Oregon. 1968-1970, Liberal Arts Major.

REFERENCES PROVIDED UPON REQUEST

SUZANNA M. RENAULT

389 KING COURT
SPRINGFIELD, MA 01101
413 555-2938

OBJECTIVE

An associate-level position in a Public Relations firm.

EXPERIENCE

Production Director, Cable Newscenter 7
Cable News Network, Springfield, MA, 1980-present
Supervise the development and airing of a one-hour cable news show. Edit video footage. Handle all video while on air. Develop and maintain strong communication with director, creating consistency in the show's format. Provide support in maintaining the flow of material.

Operations Engineer, WHHH-TV
Massachusetts Broadcasting Company, Springfield, MA, 1975-80
Provide technical support and assistance for morning and mid-morning news and commercial breaks, both local and network.

Public Relations Assistant, TIC AM/FM Cable
Springfield College, Springfield, MA, 1974-75
Supervised the public image presented by radio station. Organized a Charity Bowl-a-thon, which raised $2,000 for the Children's Care Center of Springfield. Produced and co-wrote an audio documentary about radio for local high school students. Developed and distributed press releases for all station activities. Acted as mediator during internal conflict.

EDUCATION

Bachelor of Arts, Speech Communication, University of Massachusetts, Amherst, 1974
  Hannah Tober Scholarship for student showing greatest potential in the field of Communications Management, 1974

Coursework, Television/Radio and Broadcast Journalism, University of Massachusetts, Amherst, 1979

REFERENCES AVAILABLE ON REQUEST

DONNA SAWYER COLLINS • 3890 Park Avenue • Chicago, IL 60607 • 312 555-2998

OBJECTIVE

A Position in a Federal or State Agency Involving Administration and Project Management

SKILLS HIGHLIGHTS

Management:
Program and project management, staff supervision, budget preparation and administration, public relations, staff development, human resources recruitment and selection, union contract interpretation and administration, Affirmative Action and EEO compliance planning and administration

Communication:
Team building, employee relations counseling, dispute resolution and mediation, public speaking, report writing, group facilitation

Financial:
Financial analysis, cash flow analysis, securities analysis, business and economic forecasting, project feasibility analysis, market analysis

Computer:
Prime Mainframe, IBM, Macintosh, Lotus 1-2-3, Excel, Statview, 1-2-3 Forecast, WordPerfect, and MS Word

PROFESSIONAL EXPERIENCE

Consultant, Hoffman & Monroe, Inc., Chicago, IL, 1980-present
Providing business consulting services which include market analysis, marketing planning, strategic planning, public relations, and budgeting. Projects: Market research and business planning; human resources consulting regarding EEO and Affirmative Action guidelines, hiring strategies and practices; statistical analysis; and project planning and administration

Partner, Sawyer, Collins & Co., Inc., Chicago, IL, 1970-1980
Principal in firm providing marketing analysis and planning, business forecasting and planning, and financial analysis for private firms and corporations

EDUCATION

B.A., Business Administration and Management, University of Chicago, IL, 1970

REFERENCES AVAILABLE ON REQUEST

Daniela A. Jamas

71 S.W. 15th Street • Sacramento, California 95814 • 916 555-7321 (D) • 916 555-4415 (E)

Objective: A staff management position in a human resources firm or in a corporate human resources department.

Related Experience and Skills

- Developed and provided one-day seminars and a ten-week adult education class in social services advocacy through Pacific Community College.
- Experienced with group participation, lecture, and one-on-one instructional techniques.
- Supervised a staff of ten to develop community-wide needs assessment; set training goals and objectives; developed an audience-appropriate curriculum; coordinated speaker schedule; evaluated training results.
- Tutored middle-school students with special needs on a one-on-one basis.
- Coordinated social services to help individuals meet their needs for support, counseling, resources, and information on other support services.
- Worked closely with government, private social service agencies, and businesses to integrate services that best met individual needs.
- Implemented, produced, and edited various newsletters; wrote articles for several magazines.
- Familiar with IBM computers, well versed in Macintosh word processing and database programs.
- Semi-fluent with both written and spoken Spanish.

Work History

- *Office Manager,* Environmental Consultants, Inc., Sacramento, CA, 1989-present
- *Marketing Director,* All Season Windows, Sacramento, CA, 1985-1987
- *Telemarketing Director,* Raymond Bros., Inc., San Jose, CA, 1983-1985
- *Manager,* The Book Cover, San Jose, CA, 1980-1983
- *Manager, Information and Referral,* Department of Public Affairs, Sacramento, CA, 1976-1980
- *Teacher's Aide,* Highland View Middle School, San Jose, CA, 1975-1976

Education

San Jose State University, B.S., 1976
Recreation and Leisure Studies, with an emphasis in English

References available upon request

ANNA GUPTA
3892 Barbary Road
Sacramento, CA 95813
916-555-9283

OBJECTIVE:
Buyer/Manager for an independent bookstore

EDUCATION:

1970   M.L.S.   University of Washington, Seattle

1965   B.A., Comparative   University of California, Berkeley
        Literature

PROFESSIONAL EXPERIENCE:

1980-   *Director, Media Services*
present   West Sacramento School District

           Direct the library services of twenty elementary, middle,
           and high schools in district. Supervise ten professionals
           and three para-professionals. Designed the high school
           library media center of 50,000 print and non-print items.

1975-1979 *Head Librarian*
           Berryman School Library, Sacramento, California

           Directed the acquisitions and functioning of this school
           library servicing 1,200 students and 95 professionals.
           Supervised five para-professionals.

1970-1975 *Acquisitions Librarian*
           Timberland Regional Library, Olympia, Washington

           Served as acquisitions librarian for this regional branch
           of libraries.

1965-1970 *Teacher, Literature and Writing*
           St. Mary's Girls Academy, Olympia, Washington

           Taught literature and writing courses to high school
           students at this private high school.

1962-1965 *Bookseller*
           Everyone's Books, Berkeley, California

           Part-time work while completing my degree at UC Berkeley.
           Worked as sales clerk, selling books, stocking, assisting
           customers with special orders, and receiving shipments.

REFERENCES AVAILABLE ON REQUEST

Alfred D. Landers
728 Bolero Court
Novato, CA 94945
415 555-2943

Objective

To play an integral role on a pastoral care team in a hospital or mental health facility.

Education

Training Center for Spiritual Directors, Taos Benedictine Abbey, New Mexico, 1992. Intensive
        initiation into the art of spiritual direction.
Healing Ministries, Institute of Ministries, San Jose, CA, 1989-1991.
        Formation and Advanced training, four semesters.
Clinical Pastoral Education, Mental Health Western Coast Hospital, San Jose, CA, 1988-1990.
        Internship, four units.
University of California, Santa Barbara, B.A., Psychology and Business, 1965.

Pastoral Experience

1992-1993—Community Member, Taos Benedictine Abbey
        Participated in counseling and prayer ministry with retreatants; participated in
        liturgies, retreats, and business office activities. Will complete training with an
        additional month-long program next year.
1989-1992—Chaplain intern, Western Coast Hospital
        Pastoral focus on Mentally Ill Legal Offenders. Provided Eucharist ministry to
        patients in medical, surgical, neurological, geriatric, and adult psychiatric units.
        Participated in liturgy and prayer services. Provided pastoral interviews and
        counseling, including many religious denominations and non-denominational.

Job History

1978-present—Senior Commercial Lines Underwriter, Umbrella Insurance, Group Department, San
        Rafael, CA
        Handle Oil Jobbers program in commercial group department, a nationwide
        program with heavy casualty, property, and inland marine coverage. Responsible
        for six states totaling in excess of $6 million annual premiums. Implemented
        company changes in underwriting practices and procedures. Developed 10-step
        program for profit. Audited current files.
1970-1978—Personal Lines Underwriting Supervisor, Umbrella Insurance, CA
1965-1970—Property and Casualty Underwriter, Umbrella Insurance, NJ

References upon request

Maria Nelson
226 Highline #299
Albuquerque, NM 87102
505/555-3872

Objective

A management position in television or radio advertising in which my marketing and management experience can make a strong contribution to the organization as a whole.

Work Experience

Seven-Eleven, Albuquerque, NM
Regional Marketing Director, 1989-present
Developed a successful marketing campaign for a convenience store chain. Implemented marketing strategies to increase sales by 23 percent at the least profitable outlets. Initiated and maintained a positive working relationship with radio and print media representatives. Designed a training program for store managers and staff.

Arizona Register, Phoenix, AZ
Advertising Sales, 1984-1989
Sold space advertising to a variety of business and organizational clients. Maintained excellent communications with top clients. Made cold calls on businesses to encourage advertising. Responsible for 25 percent increase in regular advertiser base over four-year period. Coordinated with design and production departments to maintain quality in advertising products as client advocate.

Arizona Evening Herald, Phoenix, AZ
Classified Advertising Sales, 1980-1984
Sold classified advertising to private and business clients. Entered advertisements in computer system. Checked advertisements for accuracy. Billed clients for advertising. Made follow-up calls to increase run of advertising. Coordinated with advertising department on special issue discount offers in the classified section.

Other work experience includes advertising sales manager for student radio station, University of Arizona; sales clerk for women's clothing boutique; and door-to-door sales representative for children's books.

Education

University of Arizona, Phoenix, AZ
Bachelor of Science in Business, 1980. Major: Advertising and Marketing.
Minor: Communications.
Honors Project Award for advertising campaign developed for student radio station
Dean's Honor Roll
Sigma Delta Gamma, advertising honorary

Seminars

Marketing Strategies in Advertising, 1992
Cooperative Advertising: Opportunities for the 1990s, Arizona Press Association, 1989

References available on request

ROBERT L. WILSON JR.

ADDRESS 1854 South Franklin Ave., Chicago, IL 60647. (312) 555-8376

OBJECTIVE A position with a literary arts center or arts advocacy agency.

EXPERIENCE

10/88 - 3/93 **Week's Worth Magazine,** Lake Zurich, IL.
Editor and Designer. Started weekly arts, culture, and entertainment magazine, gaining a circulation base of 14,000 within four months. Managed all aspects of marketing and promotion. Supervised advertising department staff for ad sales and self-promotion advertising campaigns. Managed all aspects of production. Assigned staff articles and edited free-lance articles for publication. Designed magazine from cover to cover. Managed budget and payroll for 15-person staff. Sold magazine to major publishing company.

4/86 - 9/88 **Friday's Magazine,** Illinois Daily News, Normal IL.
Editor. Assigned and edited staff stories. Created page layout and design. Wrote feature-length stories. Managed budget and 8-person staff for weekly entertainment magazine supplement to college newspaper.

8/83 - 4/86 **College of Arts and Sciences,** Illinois State University, Normal, IL.
Newsletter Editor. Created 8-page newsletter. Interviewed faculty and student leaders. Wrote feature stories. Managed all aspects of production, including photography. Handled distribution network.

8/80 - 4/86 **Illinois Daily News,** Normal, IL.
Feature Writer and Columnist. Covered various entertainment events, wrote feature stories and weekly commentary column for Features department.

1/75 - 5/80 **Communications Department,** Illinois State University, Normal, IL.
Staff Writer. Community Relations Department. Assisted in the writing, design, and layout of a 12- to 24-page alumni newsletter.

EDUCATION **B.A. Communications (Fine Arts Minor),** Illinois State University, Normal, IL, 1975.

HONORS

Critical Film Review Award, Second Place, Illinois College Press Association
Graphic Illustration Award, Second Place, Illinois College Press Association
Public Relations Society of America

REFERENCES AND PORTFOLIO AVAILABLE UPON REQUEST

GEORGETTE ANDERSON
389 Spring Rock Road
Missoula, MT 59806
(406) 555-2009

OBJECTIVE
A position in Human Resources Management for a manufacturing corporation

QUALIFICATIONS

- Design systems for recruiting, selecting, and training clerical, production, and middle management personnel
- Maintain and direct recruitment, selection, and training of those personnel
- Develop, monitor, and implement EEO/AA policy and Affirmative Action Plan
- Investigate and process complaints relating to EEO/AA
- Develop corporate policy manual on EEO/AA
- Conduct EEO/AA seminars and presentations

WORK HISTORY

Publicity Manager, Rocky Mountain Products, Missoula, MT, 1983-present.

Hired as first Communications Manager of this wood products company to develop and implement a public relations effort.

Assistant Personnel Manager, Rocky Mountain Products, Missoula, MT 1978-1983.

Assisted in recruitment, selection, and training of clerical, production, and management personnel.

Assistant Manager, Corporate EEO Programs, U.S. West Communications, Richmond, VA, 1970-1978.

Shared responsibility with corporate EEO/AA Officer for monitoring equal employment opportunity and affirmative action activities for 95 corporate locations nationwide.

EDUCATION

B.A. Communications, 1967, Mary Baldwin College, Virginia

Portfolio and references available upon request

Amelia Nelson
1545 Arboretum Drive, Apt. 34
Rutland, Vermont 05701
802-555-3828

OBJECTIVE

A corporate position in sales that involves extensive customer contact

WORK
EXPERIENCE

Public Relations Assistant
APPLEBURY INC., Burlington, Vermont, 1989-present.
• Direct interface with clients and the public, assessing needs and providing solutions. Assist in product inquiries and setting up discounting programs for qualified customers. Represent company in trade shows. Exhibit strong product knowledge in handling customer complaints through analysis and evaluation of complaint report. Support for sales force and on-site technicians.

Management/Marketing Assistant
DIVAN MANAGEMENT, Rutland, Vermont, 1979-89.
• Assisted marketing research projects and conducted a general management survey for mini-warehouse industry. Coordinated promotional campaigns, utilizing database analysis to focus on target market.

Special Promotion Assistant, Sideline Sales
UNIVERSITY BOOKSTORE, Burlington, Vermont, 1976-79.
• Responsible for selecting, ordering, and promoting the sales of sportswear to organizations and a student body of 40,000 students, over $75,000 in sales. Demonstrated skills in leadership, organization, and group motivation.

Entrepreneur
NELSON PROMOTIONS, Burlington, Vermont, 1973-75.
• Sold custom-made sportswear to Greek system and dormitories. Examined and evaluated on- and off-campus markets thorough on-site observations and informal interviews. Supervised two employees.

EDUCATION

B.A., 1973, Business and Marketing,
University of Vermont, Burlington

REFERENCES AVAILABLE ON REQUEST

Peter L. Laarsen • 3890 Peach Road • Atlanta, Georgia 30304 • 404 555-9888

Objective: A position in the manufacturing industry that will utilize my extensive background in sales and sales management.

Summary of Qualifications

Results-oriented sales professional recognized for ability to develop and maintain productive long-term relationships with clients.

Excellent track record of establishing new sales territories and attracting new clients.

Expertise in developing effective long-range marketing plans.

Strong training and motivational skills, as demonstrated by the success achieved in developing successful sales teams.

Outstanding public speaker with the proven ability to conduct effective and persuasive seminars and presentations.

Successful at projecting accurate sales and budget forecasts.

Experience

1980-present	U.S. Flyers, Chatham County Airport, Georgia **Assistant Director/Ground School Manager** Develop student enrollment for career flight academy. Utilize direct mail, telemarketing, and direct sales approaches to cultivate and qualify prospective students. Develop relationships with beneficial markets. Present promotional talks and seminars at job fairs, college campuses, and civic organizations. Act as liaison between students and school administrators. Monitor students' programs to ensure completion within designated time and budget parameters.
1977-1980	Workshops, INC., Atlanta, Georgia **Sales Director** Developed direct mail, sales plans, and marketing/advertising promotions for training workshops. Created and implemented sales training programs. Analyzed sales promotion efforts and developed new strategies. Expanded client base, securing several key corporate accounts. Increased business by 20 percent during the first year.
1973-1977	Sales Corporation of Tallahassee, Florida **Sales Trainer** Organized and presented sales training seminars.
1968-1973	U.S. Navy, Miami, Florida **Midshipman** Served on Commanding and Executive Officers staff. Awarded Sailor of the Month and Quarter.

Education

Bachelor of Business Administration, NROTC, 1968
Memphis State University, Memphis, Tennessee

Dale Carnegie Institute, 1975-1976
Awarded: Achievement, Human Relations Award; Special Award for Achievement; and Highest Award of Achievement

Activities and Awards

- Chair, Membership and Marketing Committee, Atlanta Country Club, 1984-85
- Member, City Country Club, 1980-85
- Fundraising Team, Atlanta Performing Arts, 1982-85.

References Available on Request

Susan L. Jeffers // 2235 S.W. Hammond // Laramie, Wyoming 82057 // 307/555-9872

Career Goal

Communications Director in a corporate environment

Demonstrated Skills

Experienced with marketing and public relations—developing marketing strategies and campaigns, dealing with sensitive issues with the news media, and developing and projecting an organization's most positive image.

Ability to develop plans, goals, strategies, and timelines, and to maintain schedules and analyze the results of projects.

Ability to work independently and exercise sound judgment.

Excellent communications skills, both in writing and in making public presentations to small and large groups on a variety of topics.

Ability to work effectively with the public, elected officials, board and committee members, program operators, and staff in a teamwork environment.

Experienced in grant writing and fund-raising.

Thorough knowledge of state and federal government operations and regulations affecting business in the state.

Experienced with preparation and production of graphics materials, including brochures, newsletters, and annual reports.

Knowledge of newspaper advertising department practices in advertising sales, placement, and design.

Professional Experience

Research Specialist, Public Relations Department, State of Wyoming
June 1984 to present

Advertising Sales, Laramie Evening News, Wyoming
January 1982 to May 1984

Advertising Production, Sheridan Sun, Sheridan, Wyoming
August 1978 to November 1981

Advertising Intern, Laramie Evening News, Wyoming
June to August 1978

Education

B.A. in Journalism/Advertising, University of Wyoming, Laramie, 1978
Won AASA award for design of print advertising campaign

references are available upon request

Arthur Lewis
789 Hansborough Street
Boston, Massachusetts 02169
617 555-8962

objective   to find employment in a human services field which offers new challenges and opportunities and utilizes the experience, skills, and knowledge from nearly 20 years of increasing responsibility in the education field.

specific strengths

creativity   ability to synthesize diverse ideas into coherent concepts; ability to think in new directions; ability to assist others in more clearly stating their ideas and objectives

tolerance   ability to work with a diverse population and enjoy the interaction and challenges of diversity; essentially team-oriented and a "people" person

assessment   ability to employ various standard and non-standard assessment processes as well as mature insight in the evaluation of programs and proposals

writing   ability to write informally and formally, imaginatively as well as in a scholarly, more research-directed style

speaking   ability to present difficult and challenging concepts in formal oral presentations; strong small group skills and experience; significant teaching ability with diverse student population

education
M.A., Education, 1973, University of Massachusetts, Boston, MA.
B.A., African American Studies and American Literature, 1970,
Boston University, Boston, MA.

employment history

Language Arts Department Head, Jamaica Plain High School, Jamaica Plain, MA. 1988-present. Coordinated curriculum planning and implementation. Acted as department liaison to school board and administration. Taught English, Creative Writing, Technical and Research Writing, American Literature, British Literature, and Multicultural Literature. Supervised the production and publication of a student literary magazine.

English and Writing Instructor, Jamaica Plain High School, Jamaica Plain, MA. 1980-1988. Taught English, Creative Writing, Technical and Research Writing, American Literature, British Literature, Multicultural Literature, and Speech to high school students. Tutored remedial and advanced students of Literature and Writing. Served as faculty sponsor of African American Student Union.

Language Arts Instructor, Franklin Junior High School, West Roxbury, MA. 1975-1980. Taught English, Reading, Speech, and Writing classes to 7th and 8th grade students. Faculty sponsor and advisor for the Student Drama Group.

Substitute Teacher, South Boston Districts, Boston, MA. 1973-1975. Taught Language Arts classes in junior and senior high schools in South Boston.

references available on request

MARYANNE BARBARAS
38549 Palm Lane
Hialeah, Florida 33010
(305) 555-3088

OBJECTIVE

To utilize proven skills in planning and managing programs and employees to help a children's advocacy organization plan and manage its services.

EXPERIENCE

Manager, Customer Support, Peyton Products, Inc., Hialeah, Florida, 1986-present
MAJOR ACCOMPLISHMENTS:
* Reorganized and combined the Manufacturing Order Service Department and Sales Customer Service Department into customer-sensitive customer support group.
* Developed procedures, systems, and a team concept to better utilize skills and talents while increasing productivity.
* Designed WORK program to promote a "quality of service" approach to customer relations.
* Coordinated the conversion of a new order system as well as participated in the formal design of the integrated sales/manufacturing system.
* Developed various inventory programs and systems to increase responsiveness to customer product requirements.
* Implemented programs designed to increase staff motivation to achieve positive growth through goal setting and recognition.
* Managed a budget of approximately one million dollars.
* Managed a staff of twenty professionals and nonprofessionals.

Manager, Order Service, Peyton Products, Inc., Hialeah, Florida, 1975-1985
MAJOR ACCOMPLISHMENTS:
* Reorganized the three domestic and international order service product groups into one organization.
* Developed unifying procedures and a cooperative working environment.
* Developed closer interdepartmental alignment, improving production scheduling to meet customer product requirements.
* Developed closer interdepartmental alignment with the customer service group to improve order/production status reporting for improved customer relations.
* Increased staff development activity through conference attendance, advanced degree encouragement, and product group team leadership.

Customer Service Representative, Peyton Products, Inc., Hialeah, Florida, 1972-1975

Teacher, Lincoln Middle School, Tampa, Florida, 1966-1970

EDUCATION

Columbia University Graduate School, September 1972
Two-Year Seminar/Certification, Market Analysis for Competitive Advantage

Florida State University, 1966
Bachelor of Arts, History

REFERENCES AVAILABLE UPON REQUEST

JEAN HANAKA

3829 Deering Street, Apt. 23A • Portland, Maine 04101 • 207~555~2483

Objective:

A position as staff photographer for a public relations firm or university communications department.

Education:

B.F.A., Photography, New England Institute of Art, Maine, 1992.
Coursework in Art and Photography, South Central Community College, Buffalo, New York, 1970-1971.
B.S., Liberal Studies, Plainfield College, Plainfield, Vermont, 1969.

Professional Experience:

1981-present, Office Coordinator, Community Relations Office, University of Southern Maine, Portland, Maine
  Produce educational and promotional material (copy and photos) for many campus events and displays, both on and off campus. Write advertising copy for both radio and newspapers. Design and assist in designing advertising layout for newspapers. Establish and reorganize procedures for maintaining records, billings, and follow-up; organize detailed record-keeping for the Speaker's Service; initiate surveys and tabulation of area rental rooms, prices, and contact persons. Write office guidelines, including an office procedures manual. Maintain campus maps, staff directory, and new employee packets. Monitor and assign work to four classified staff and supervise three to six work-study students.

1979-1981, Senior Secretary, Community Relations Office, University of Southern Maine, Portland, Maine
  Assisted the Community Relations Director. Maintained office records. Coordinated room reservations, Speakers' Service functions, and assignments for the Graphics area of the CRO.

1971-1979, Staff Photographer, Learning Resource Center, Buffalo, New York
  Provided photographs for LRC Newsletter, bi-annual bulletin, and promotion and publicity use. Researched community events, local news, and trends for news and photography leads. Attended all LRC events. Completed layouts of newsletter and bulletin.

Portfolio and references available upon request

RAOUL HARMON
910 NE 223rd #987 • Brooklyn, New York 11201 • 718-555-2909

Objective

A position in the Promotions Department of a Publishing House

Work Experience

Customer Service Assistant, 1987-present, Academic Book Service, Inc., Brooklyn, NY
- Research problems with library book shipments using custom C-Basic database, searching both archived records and current orders with publishers.
- Prepare documentation for library book returns for credit, and reorder correct books when required.
- Contact publishers for price and availability information regarding library orders.
- Determine type of credit issued, securing evidence involving discrepancies with library orders and actual books received.

Book Purchasing Clerk and Sales and Promotion Assistant, 1980-1987, Blue Water Gallery and Shop, New York, NY
- Responsible for book ordering and stocking.
- Assisted with merchandising.
- Assisted with production of publicity materials (fliers, signs, posters, invitations).
- Responsible for customer service and sales.

Senior Editor, 1972-1980, Blackman East, Inc., Newark, NJ
- Proofread and compared academic and public libraries' Series Authority file records against Library of Congress' Authority file to standardize catalogued records.
- Edited records and bibliographic files using Basic language on an IBM terminal.
- Researched problem headings and series updates.

Education

- B.A. 1971, City College of New York, NY
  Philosophy and Literature
  Assistant Editor of student literary magazine

References

Available upon request

Sandra B. Walters
334 Northwest Vineland Avenue • Concord, New Hampshire 03321 • 603.555-2214

Career Interest: Outward Bound Instructor in Mountain Climbing Division.

Important Skills & Experience:

• First American woman to climb Tengeboche Himal in Nepal.
• Completed solo 1,000 mile trek in Chilean Andes.
• Made ascent to 21,000-foot elevation on Everest before weather ended expedition.
• Climbed seven major peaks in the Cascade Mountain Range in Oregon and Washington.
• Organized and led climbs to four major peaks in Rocky Mountains in Colorado and Wyoming.
• Organized and led treks on the Pacific Crest Trail from Canada to Mexico.
• Wrote book (as yet unpublished) on experiences trekking in Third World countries.

Related Work Experience:

• Taught high school history in public schools for 12 years.
• Provided counseling assistance in program for drug-dependent youth.
• Taught short courses in backpacking and mountain climbing for local sporting goods store.
• Taught courses and led trips for university student outdoor recreation center.

Employment History:

History Teacher, South Concord High School, September 1984 to June 1992
History Teacher, Washington Lee High School, Boston, September 1980 to June 1984

Additional Work Experience:

Real Estate Sales, Central Home Realty, Boston, 1974 to 1980
Secretary, Central Home Realty, Boston, 1972 to 1974

Education:

Coursework in Counseling, University of New Hampshire, 1990-1992
B.A., History, Boston University, 1980

References available on request

WANDA ELAINE FARBER
14 East First Street
Wichita, Kansas 67231
316.555-6129

GOAL:

Develop a challenging career in sales leading to management in marketing and sales.

PREVIOUS EXPERIENCE:

Office Manager, Martin Accounting, Inc., Wichita, Kansas, 1988 to present

Handle all bookkeeping and office staff personnel responsibilities. Maintain payroll and ledger sheets. Monitor employee productivity and activity reports. Review actual expenditures and income periodically in accordance with budgeted figures. Work with owner to develop planning and financial reports.

Gift Shop Sales Clerk, St. Joseph's Hospital, Wichita, Kansas, 1982 to 1987

Responsible for stocking inventory, making and recording sales, balancing daily receipts, and closing gift shop after hours. Provided assistance to hospital visitors seeking gifts and greeting cards for patients. Responded to queries from nursing staff and doctors. Delivered floral bouquets as required.

Cashier, Wal-Mart, Wichita, Kansas, 1978 to 1982

Trained new employees on cashier's responsibilities and procedures. Made sales, recorded transactions, and balanced cash drawer at end of shift. Assisted with restocking. Answered questions for store patrons.

Childcare Provider, Little Ones Day Care Center (Self-Employed), Marquette, Iowa, 1968 to 1978

Started private day care center with two employees caring for fourteen children, ages 18 months to 5 years. Developed and implemented pre-school curriculum for older children. Provided informational newsletter to parents of children in the center.

EDUCATION:

Continuing Education, Falls City Community College, Wichita, Kansas
    Completed 14 credit hours in Marketing through the Business Department; currently enrolled in Management Systems and Finance.

Associate's Degree, Business, Central Community College, Cedar Rapids, Iowa
    Coursework focused on business management, finance, and accounting.

REFERENCES:

Available on request.

Stephan Monetti
34 South Avon Street
Charleston, South Carolina 29411
603.555-2236

Career Objective

Senior Manager leading to Project Director position

Career Achievements

Direct, supervise, and administer turn-key projects from inception to start-up for equipment manufacturing firm.

Coordinate with sales department to review system process design, equipment sizes, schedule, and engineering costs before presenting final proposal to the client.

Negotiate purchases and advise corporate president and CEO of pending contracts and negotiations.

Completed seventeen domestic projects and twenty international projects in Latin America, South America, Spain, and Africa.

Conceived, initiated, and successfully sold design of two new equipment products that resulted in a 40 percent increase in corporate sales over two years.

Completed all projects on or ahead of schedule. All projects resulted in corporate profits; many produced higher profits than anticipated.

Instituted procedures for project document handling and project communication.

Trained project engineers and project managers to design and manage assigned projects.

Instituted program for college interns and developed training program that culminated in job offers to those graduates whose performance met challenges of the position. After seven years, all students thus hired are still with the company and highly productive.

Supervise four project management teams, including twelve engineers and sixteen draftsmen.

Acted as site project engineer during construction of $250 million plant.

Registered professional engineer in the states of South Carolina and Arkansas.

Career Experience

Senior Project Manager, DRG Inc., Charleston, South Carolina, 1978-present
Senior Project and Process Engineer, Hopewell Systems, Charleston, 1974-78
Process and Plant Engineer, Wembley Haddon, Inc., Little Rock, Arkansas, 1972-74
Consultant Engineer, Toverston Dryers, Little Rock, 1971-72
Pilot Plant and Process Development Engineer, James River Corp., Neenah, Wisconsin, 1967-71

Education

M.S. Chemical Engineering, Georgia Institute of Technology, Atlanta, 1978
B.S. Engineering, University of Wisconsin, Milwaukee, 1967

Professional References Available as Requested

Toby Allan Willis
22367 Madrigal Way
Bakersfield, California 93326
(805) 555-2345

Career Objective

A management position in a growing corporate firm that will maximize my proven abilities in:
Administrative Management • Corporate Affairs • Public and Community Relations

Skills and Experience

Recruited, trained, and developed management teams of up to 15.

Held direct supervisory responsibility for up to 2,500 employees.

Successfully prepared and administered operating and capital budgets totaling $355 million.

Oversaw all operating functions associated with capital improvement projects totaling $200 million.

Initiated operations analysis used as the basis for creating corporate management plan.

Supervised development of business plan that reduced operating costs by $750,000.

Guided operations analyses, resulting in significant efficiency improvements and cost savings.

Implemented changes to work processes and operating procedures, including upgrade of management methods and systems and reallocation of personnel resources.

Devised and implemented corporate reorganization that resulted in centralization of key services.

Handled all aspects of corporate relations for multi-million-dollar corporation.

Introduced coordinated management reporting system which yielded significant gains in internal/external communications, management decision making, and organizational efficiency.

Adapted existing budget from cost accounting to accrual/modified zero-base budgeting system.

Worked with businesses and corporations to foster expansion and improved competitiveness.

Developed public relations program that involved print and broadcast advertising, network marketing at official meetings and conferences, and public presentations to corporate boards.

Created, implemented, and tested a marketing program successful in establishing a new company's identity and product recognition through a five-state service area.

Employment History

Chief Executive Officer, City of Santa Rosa, California, 1988 to present

General Manager, City of Pueblo, Colorado, 1986 to 1988

Vice President of Marketing and Public Relations, Workman Group, Denver, Colorado, 1980 to 1986

Previous employment represents progressive general management and public relations positions in private-sector corporations in Colorado and Virginia.

Education

M.M.A., Management and Administration, Willamette University, Salem, Oregon, 1974

B.S. Business Administration, Bridgeport University, Connecticut, 1970

References provided on request

TONYA W. HARDING
3890 WEST 43rd AVE
DETROIT, MICHIGAN 48106
313 • 555 • 3892

CAREER OBJECTIVE

Senior managerial position in financial analysis or strategic marketing department

ACHIEVEMENTS

- Designed a marketing strategy which resulted in a 20 percent increase in sales.
- Directed equipment upgrades that resulted in new business sales of 20 percent.
- Increased profits 20 percent through pricing control and productivity improvements.
- Designed corporate strategy that resulted in major reorganization.
- Completed sale of one plant, representing $20 million.
- Established the long-range marketing strategy for the Stratton Brothers Corporation.
- Developed a corporate identity campaign which broadened Stratton Brothers' national scope.
- Managed $50 million of contracts for tissue products.
- Increased profitability of products as a result of involvement in planning and introduction of new technologies.
- Improved productivity and quality improvements involving twenty professional and technical personnel.
- Supervised thirty professional and technical personnel in three departments.

EMPLOYMENT SUMMARY

STRATTON BROTHERS CORPORATION, 1982-CURRENT
A $1 billion public corporation serving paper and tissue products markets.
Vice President, Detroit, Michigan, 1989-CURRENT
Catalog and Services Group. Direct sales, marketing, customer services, estimating, and distribution for a two-plant, $125 million sales operation.
Assistant Vice President, Detroit, Michigan, 1982-1989
Directed sales and marketing for five departments in main plant.

PULLMAN PRODUCTS, INC., 1969-1982
A $800 million market leader in consumer sanitary products.
Director of Corporate Development, Ypsilanti, Michigan, 1981-1982
Manager of Product Engineering, Ypsilanti, Michigan, 1977-1981
Operations Manager, Ypsilanti, Michigan, 1973-1976
Manager of Production Control, Ypsilanti, Michigan, 1969-1972

EDUCATION

University of Michigan, Grand Rapids, 1969, M.S., Industrial Technology

University of Kansas, Topeka, 1967, B.S., Mechanical Engineering, Business Minor

REFERENCES UPON REQUEST

JONATHAN BENCHLEY III.
515 West 57th, No. 126
New York, NY 10512
212/555-2352

Employment Objective: Production Supervisor for a corporate advertising department.

Professional Work Experience

1985 - present
Jefferson Medical Group, New York, NY
PUBLICATIONS COORDINATOR
Wrote, edited, and submitted articles to professional medical journals and trade publications regarding treatment procedures and research findings. Prepared and maintained research records system. Wrote news releases and designed and prepared brochures and monthly newsletter. Coordinated all aspects of production and printing for brochures, newsletter, and two books written by staff doctors.

1978 - 1984
The Science Record, Columbia University, New York, NY
EDITOR
Interviewed, wrote, edited, proofread, and designed *The Science Record*, a quarterly magazine published by the College of Science at Columbia University. Prepared brochures. Helped plan and organize a conference of medical scientists and coordinated production and publication of the resultant book. Edited and coordinated production for a three-volume treatise on medical developments in the Soviet Union.

1975 - 1978
New York Times, New York, NY
DISPLAY ADVERTISING PRODUCTION
Designed ad layouts, created artwork, created promotional ads, produced art boards, sold advertising. Handled production department in absence of production manager. Maintained advertising records and originals storage.

1970 - 1975
Starker Printing, Inc., Long Island, NY
PRODUCTION STAFF
Handled newspaper and magazine layouts for a variety of clients. Learned processes for all phases of production: mock-up, typesetting, copy fitting, darkroom camera operation, stripping, plate making, and press operation.

Education
City College, New York, NY
A.A. Degree, Graphic Design, 1975
A.A. Degree, Printing and Production Technology, 1969

Professional References Available on Request

Olivia G. Sumner – 12 Wabash Ave. – Knoxville, TN 37982 – 615-555-8974

Objective

A management position in public/customer relations that will challenge my organizational, communication, and planning skills.

Professional Skills and Achievements

Developed major promotional campaign for increasing advertising revenues; coordinated sales for special-issue display and classified advertising sections.

Served as personal liaison to advertising agencies throughout the state; made effective sales presentations and secured new accounts.

Planned work flow assignments to successfully meet all established deadlines and management objectives; interacted effectively with all departments to provide highest levels of efficiency and to maintain excellent standards of customer service.

Oversaw quality performance for customer service, public relations, and clerical activities; provided troubleshooting for complex and/or sensitive customer problems.

Organized and directed all company office activities, including interviewing, hiring, training, scheduling, and supervising office support personnel; oversaw counseling on employee benefits plans, assisted with claims; established and maintained compliance to state reporting regulations.

Assisted Controller with cash management and other financial duties, including control and distribution of accounts payable. Made wire transfers of account funds. Assisted in bank finance negotiations.

Reviewed and verified company credit applications and set credit limits for clients.

Developed and recommended appropriate changes in credit policy. Processed and authorized orders and invoices; credited account payments and tracked past due amounts. Sent late notices; negotiated customer payment arrangements for collection of delinquent account balances; initiated legal procedures as required.

Made direct contact with customers and prospective clients; maintained highest possible customer service standards. Maintained current knowledge of sales and special promotional events; served as support and backup for marketing/sales force. Provided customers with general and technical product information and special assistance. Promptly resolved order and/or account problems; ensured that orders were received; interacted effectively with other company departments; tracked order shipments through contact with freight company representatives.

Conducted customer research projects to help improve service policies.

Employment History

Office Manager, Tennessee Medical Association, Knoxville, 1985-present
Credit & Collection Manager, Tennessee Medical Association, Knoxville, 1981-85
Customer Service Manager, Tennessee Medical Association, Knoxville, 1974-81
Cost Accountant, Tennessee Medical Association, Knoxville, 1973-74
Sales/Office Support Staff, Knoxville Gazette, 1970-73

Education & Training

B.A. Public Administration, 1991, University of Tennessee, Knoxville
A.A., Business, 1979, Knoxville Central College, Knoxville, Tennessee

References Provided on Request

MAIA JOINER • 24 Wellington Place • Tallahassee, Florida • 904-555-6787

OBJECTIVE
A position in a Public Relations firm or department.

EXPERIENCE

Production Engineer, Channel 5 News at Noon
Tallahassee, Florida   1983-present
- Supervise the development and airing of a one-hour cable news show.
- Produce and edit video footage for self-promotion spots and special programming.
- Handle all on air commercial breaks.
- Develop and maintain strong communication with director.
- Assure continued consistency in the show's format.
- Provide support in maintaining the flow of material.

Operations Engineer, WIRO-TV
Florida Public Broadcasting Company, Tallahassee   1980-83
- Provide technical support and assistance for morning and mid-morning news and commercial breaks, both local and network.
- Oversee camera crew of three operators and two technicians.
- Check operations of equipment; maintain reliable operating conditions.

Public Relations Associate, WJKE-FM Radio
Florida Public Broadcasting Company, Tallahassee   1978-80
- Organized a Charity Dance-a-thon, which raised $2,000 for the Children's Burn Treatment Center of Tallahassee.
- Produced and co-wrote an audio documentary about the dropout rate in local high schools.
- Developed and distributed press releases for all station activities. Acted as mediator during internal conflict.
- Produced promotional videos for airing on public television sister station.

Student Intern, WJKE-FM Radio
Florida Public Broadcasting Company, Tallahassee   1978
- Assisted with sound system testing and maintenance.
- Worked with production engineers on recording and editing programs.

EDUCATION

Bachelor of Arts, Speech Communication, 1978, Florida State University, Tallahassee
- **Coursework focus** Television/Radio and Broadcast Journalism
Bachelor of Science, Electrical Engineering, 1976, Florida State University
- **Coursework focus** Electronics and Video Technology

REFERENCES AVAILABLE ON REQUEST

Lt. Col. Jarred B. Hillman ➤ Command Unit 32, U.S. Army Base ➤ Ft. Lewis, WA 98023

➤ Career Objective
Management position with private corporation or government agency

➤ Experience

Served 26 years in military command positions, achieving the rank of Lt. Colonel in the U.S. Army.

Held active-duty commands in the Persian Gulf, Vietnam, and Berlin. Served as a Senior Aide to the Commander in Chief during Operation Desert Storm.

Supervised troop numbers up to 1,500 in war-time; up to 4,000 in peace-time operations.

Responsible for training and assignment of enlisted officers and ROTC graduates.

Served as Director of Commissary with responsibility for budgeting, planning, administration, inventory control, and staff supervision of 50 military and civilian employees.

Served as Director of Hospital Facilities with responsibility for budgeting, planning, and administration of 200-bed facility. Worked closely with military and civilian physicians to develop operations procedures for hospital.

As ROTC Sergeant, trained new recruits during orientation period.

➤ Education

Bachelor of Science, Business & Management, ROTC, Michigan State University, 1960.

➤ Military Service

Enlisted in U.S. Army Reserve Officer Training Corps 1958.
Graduated with Honors to the Rank of Second Lieutenant, 1962.
Served in Vietnam, 1962-1970. Achieved Rank of First Lieutenant.
Stationed in Berlin, East Germany, 1970-1972. Achieved Rank of Captain.
Stationed in Ft. Bliss, Texas, 1972-1978. Director of Hospital Facilities.
Transferred to Ft. Rucker, Alabama, 1978-1990. Director of Commissary Operations.
    Achieved Rank of Major, 1989.
Served in Operation Desert Storm in the Persian Gulf, 1990. Achieved Rank of Lt.
    Colonel.

Complete record of service and recommendations available upon request.

MARK K. MYERSON
7892 Fir Street SW
Tyler, Texas 75702
405/555-9371

OBJECTIVE

Seeking a position with the advertising department of a newspaper or magazine where my experience with writing, communications, and public relations may contribute to advertising sales.

PROFESSIONAL EXPERIENCE

The Quarter Horse Journal, Tyler, TX: EDITORIAL COORDINATOR, January 1987-Present
Wrote short articles, assisted with editing, proofread all editorial and advertising copy, supervised copy flow between editorial and production departments, and assisted with advertising sales.

Oklahoma Scoring Services, Norman, OK: ESSAY READER, January 1984-January 1987
Graded essays for the state GED examinations.

High School, Maysville, OK: TEACHER, August 1980-June 1984
Taught English, Journalism, Speech. Served as student yearbook and newspaper adviser.

The Southwestern, Southwestern Oklahoma State University, Weatherford, OK: REPORTER, January-June 1974; ADVERTISING SALESPERSON, January-June 1973.
Assigned articles to student reporters, wrote and edited articles for the paper, chose copy to include in each issue, assisted in layouts and headline writing. Took calls for advertising department to reserve space for advertisements, developed advertising promotion ads and flyers to encourage sales of personal and business classified ads.

Public Relations Department, Southwestern Oklahoma State University: REPORTER, September 1972-May 1973.
Conducted interviews and wrote press releases on various faculty members and students at the college to be published in local newspapers and distributed to hometown newspapers.

EDUCATION

University of Texas, Tyler, TX: Master of Arts, Journalism (Advertising), 1992
University of Oklahoma, Norman, OK: Teacher Certification, English, 1980
Southwestern Oklahoma State University, Weatherford, OK: Bachelor of Arts, Journalism, 1974

REFERENCES WILL BE FORWARDED ON REQUEST

ANTONIO CUNHA
3890 Boulevard
Los Angeles, CA 90052
213-555-4443

OBJECTIVE

A position in magazine design and production that would employ my extensive journalistic background and computer skills

COMPUTER SKILLS

- Macintosh consultant, five years
- President of Macintosh Users Group of Santa Barbara, four years
- Desktop publishing/graphics specialist, five years
- Network/Systems trainer, four years
- Troubleshooting/support services, four years
- Knowledgeable about all major graphics, desktop publishing, and word processing software for the Macintosh

EDUCATION

B.S. in Technical Journalism, University of California at Los Angeles, 1974
Coursework in Journalism at University of Hawaii, 1971-72

EXPERIENCE

EDITOR, Dean Publications, Los Angeles, 1985-present
Bi-weekly publication with 25,000 national/international circulation, and co-editing/reporting for 22,000-circulation weekly. Edit all copy, write headlines, proof, complete layout, complete graphics/photo selection, create art/graphs, operate computers, and organize/improve databases.

SPORTS REPORTER, Long Beach Times, CA, 1983-85
Daily newspaper with 156,000 circulation. Reported Pac-10 football and basketball, high school sports, various features, photography, cartoon work, and contributed to Gannett News Service.

COPY DESK, Santa Barbara Gazette, CA, 1981-83
Morning newspaper with 160,000 circulation. Completed wire and local editing, headline and cutline writing, page layout and wire photo selection.

SPORTS REPORTER, Honolulu Star-Bulletin, HI, 1975-80
Evening newspaper with 188,000 circulation. Covered Triple-A baseball (Pacific League), college and high school season and tournament play, including selection of all-star teams. Wrote features and side-bars. Edited wire and local copy. Wrote headlines and cutlines.

FREELANCE, Associated Press, Hawaii Bureau, 1971-72
Part-time assignments included coverage of Triple-A baseball and basketball tournaments.

REFERENCES AVAILABLE UPON REQUEST

KRISTINA BOUGH
P.O. Box 213
Boise, Idaho 83702
☎ 208.555.8920

OBJECTIVE: To obtain a managerial position in advertising with a magazine or newspaper

PROFESSIONAL EXPERIENCE

Advertising Director, *The Boise Sun,* Boise, ID. August 1985-present.
Responsibilities: Develop advertisements and promotions materials for advertising clients. Conduct periodic reader surveys and analyze responses with regard to demographics, marketing strategies, and subscription potential. Created ads that were directly responsible for producing $50,000 in additional advertising sales in a two-month period. Awarded two regional and one national American Newspaper Advertisers Association Honor Awards for in-house advertising design. Supervise staff of 6 advertising sales representatives and 5 graphic and production artists and typesetters.

Marketing Coordinator, Continuing Education Department, University of Idaho. 1980-1983.
Responsibilities: Plan and develop marketing strategy for attracting students to the university's Summer Term program. Write and design promotional literature, including bulletins, brochures, advertisements, and public service announcements. Coordinate with designers, typesetters, photographers, service bureaus, media advertising sales representatives, and printers. Maintain advertising and promotion budget. Conduct surveys and evaluations.

Promotion Coordinator, *InterArts Magazine,* Boise, ID. 1977-1979.
Responsibilities: Coordinate all advertising sales for 12-page display advertising section in the back of the magazine, plus 2-page classified ad section. Make customer calls, develop ad rate cards and advertiser fact sheet, handle billing and collection. Schedule self-promotion advertising and exchange advertising with other publications. Maintain advertising budget.

News Editor, *The Herald Independent,* University of Boise student newspaper. 1975-1977.
Responsibilities: Write news copy, assign news stories to student reporters. Determine editorial content of newspaper hard-news pages. Coordinate feature stories with other staff editors. Assist with layout, copyediting, and production.

EDUCATION

University of Idaho, Boise. Master of Arts. Major: Advertising. 1985. GPA 4.0.
Montana State University, Bozeman. Bachelor of Arts. Major: Journalism. 1977. GPA 3.87.

HONORS

UI Graduate Teaching Fellowship, Journalism/Advertising, 1983-1985
UI Scholar's Award, 1985
MSU Scholarship and Leadership Award, 1975, 1976, 1977
R.L. Underwood Scholarship, 1973-1977
Membership in University Honor Societies: Sigma Delta Chi and Kappa Tau Alpha
   (Journalism Honoraries), Phi Kappa Phi, Mortar Board, Alpha Lambda Delta, Talons,
   Phi Eta Sigma

REFERENCES available on request

Michael Munez
25983 Sunset Blvd.
Los Angeles, California 90049
213/555-3892

Objective: An administrative position in a social services agency which would utilize my broad experience in directing operations, human resources, and public relations.

Accomplishments

Managing
√ Directed six-state, 1,000-employee, 7 day/week, 24 hour/day operations that achieved top performance results in the nation.
√ Led the first major operator services reorganization in the U.S. after breakup of the Bell System, developing methods used around the country.
√ Conceived and implemented service improvement for calls from privately owned coin telephones resulting in a 95 percent drop in customer complaints and a 75 percent improvement in productivity.
√ Established cooperative process with union local which produced unique, "customized" work environments and was cited as exemplary by the union during 14-state bargaining.
√ Established and directed company-wide departmental quality assurance organization.
√ Redesigned employee scheduling, introducing a significant number of part-time employees and improving employee productivity.

Human Resources/Management Development
√ Developed and implemented "high risk/high reward" program for selected female managers.
√ Elected to chair Governor's Management Selection and Development Steering Committee charged with planning a management development program for state employees.
√ Selected by National Management Association to teach courses in fundamental management concepts for new and aspiring managers.
√ Recognized by AT&T for implementing one of the outstanding Initial Management Development Programs in the country.

Public Relations
√ Served as Company spokesperson to broadcast and print media.
√ Wrote monthly columns in the Company's employee and public newsletters.
√ Guest speaker for civic organizations, corporate conferences, and university classes on topics including Change, Management Development, Job Enrichment, and Corporate Public Relations.
√ Managed statewide public relations, including media relations, employee information, and video production. Edited news releases and hosted press conferences.

Employment History
Southern California Telephone Company, **Regional Operations Manager**, 1986-present.
American Telephone & Telegraph, **Human Resources Director**, 1984-1985.
Midwest Bell, **Public Relations Coordinator**, 1975-1983.

Education
Bachelor of Arts, Business Administration, University of Iowa, 1972.
Awards and Honors: Phi Beta Kappa, Abbey Foundation Award as Outstanding Business Graduate, Beta Gamma Sigma.

References available on request.

June M. Kurtz   389 West 26th
                                      New York, New York 10010
                                      212-555-2934

Objective
Seeking a position offering opportunities for advancement and career growth in the fields of Education and Economic Welfare.

Education
Master of Arts, Public Administration, City University of New York, New York, NY, 1983.
Bachelor of Arts, History and Economics, State University of New York, Albany, NY, 1972.

Professional Experience
<u>Commissioner</u>, New York County, New York, 1983-1992. Administration and management for the government of New York County with a staff of 900 employees and a population of 2,225,000. One of three commissioners serving on the Board of Commissioners.

<u>Assistant to the President</u>, Waltech Industries, Inc., Albany Sand and Gravel, Albany, New York, 1981-1983. Responsible for developing industrial land, acquisition of land, securing and filing all necessary governmental documents, and securing and administering project financing.

<u>Vice President</u>, Allen Corporation, Albany, New York, 1974-1981. Part-owner of a multi-million dollar corporation involved in the construction of subdivisions and residential houses. Employed 25 people and built approximately 36 houses per year.

Professional Affiliations and Governmental Affiliations
Chaired New York State Council of Governments
Chaired New York City Economic Development Council
Chaired New York County Economic Development Advisory Committee
Chaired Albany Parkway Citizen's Advisory Committee
Co-chaired Solid Waste Advisory Committee
Board of Directors, Jobs Council
Board of Directors, Albany Youth Drug and Alcohol Association

Additional Background
Elected to office of New York County Commissioner, New York, 1983-1992—
    Government administration and management.
Successfully initiated two international trade missions between New York City and
    Montreal, Canada, resulting in trade initiatives with Canada in 1986 and 1989.
Industrial land development.
Business administration and management in the private sector.
Business Education Teacher, Albany Senior School.
Administered the research, planning, and building of the New York County Waste
    Energy Mass Burn Plant, 1984.
Administered the planning and building of a 255- to 510-cell correctional facility, 1987.
Responsible for initiating and developing international trade between the province of
    Quebec and the state of New York.
Developed and initiated the Albany Economic Development District, 1985.
Facilitated development of Albany's first industrial park. Aided in industrial development
    areas in Buffalo.
Facilitated development of industrial lands in Albany area, including project cost
    estimations and installation plans for streets, water, sewer, and other amenities.

References available on request

Dale McIrney
• 4903 West Holly Drive • Salt Lake City, Utah 84112 • 801-555-3982 •

Objective:

A position in retail sales offering opportunities for advancement in retail management

Professional Experience:

Clerical Specialist, Utah State Hospital, Salt Lake City, Utah, 1980-present
   Duties include: maintain and update records and resource material; receive and disburse funds for Patient and Administrative accounts; prepare bank deposits and change orders; reconcile cash drawers; manage cash, filing, typing, and correspondence; operate computer; handle telephone and in-person communications with physicians, social workers, psychiatrists, patients, family members, general public, and representatives from other state agencies.

Clerical Specialist, State of Utah, Disability Determination Services, Salt Lake City, Utah, 1975-1980
   Duties included: medical transcription, case set-up, association of mail to cases, filing, production typing, maintaining and updating resource materials, correspondence, telephone communications with physicians and claimants, and coordination with other state agencies.

Customer Representative, Western Federal Bank, Salt Lake City, Utah, 1974-1975
   Duties for this temporary appointment included: customer relations, handling customer complaints and problems, correspondence, computer terminal operation, typing, maintaining customer accounts, filing, and cash handling.

Administrative Secretary, Paul D. Edwards & Co., Logan, Utah, 1970-1974
   Duties included: computer terminal operation, correspondence, typing, maintaining files, writing and placing orders, customer relations, and daily radio broadcasts.

Salesperson, Marshall T. Brawn, Logan, Utah, 1965-1967
   Duties included: assisting customers, stocking merchandise, and preparing merchandise for floor.

Education:

Merrill David Business College, Logan, Utah, 1967-1970
   Bookkeeping graduate; additional course study in secretarial sciences, medical office procedures, and retail office managing.

References provided upon request

ANDREW VIZENOR
143 NW 29TH
EVERETT, WA 98215
206 555-9283

PROFESSIONAL EMPLOYMENT OBJECTIVE

Position as public school administrator.

PROFESSIONAL EXPERIENCE

Special Program Consultant, Bethel School, Bethel, Alaska, 1990-1993. Developed and directed Attendance Incentive Program, a broad plan based on community involvement and cultural exploration. Assisted in directing community education programs developed as support for this program. Served on local Advisory Education Committee.

Classroom Teacher and Advisor, Bethel School, Bethel, Alaska, 1986-1990. Created, organized, directed, and evaluated classroom instruction in social studies, language arts, reading improvement, and science for grades 7-12. Acted as student advisor and administrative liaison for Attendance Incentive Program, student government, and chess club.

Director, Community Action Program, Seattle, Washington, 1978-1985. Developed, managed, and implemented programs for CAP, a non-profit community organization committed to providing educational and vocational opportunities, fostering cooperative community efforts to beautify and maintain neighborhoods, and involving poor youth and youth of color in community-based projects and activities. Coordinated responsibilities of staff, including an Office Manager, Assistant Director, Volunteer Coordinator, and Education Director. Planned budgets and reported to Board of Directors.

EDUCATION

Master of Education, University of Washington, Seattle, Washington, 1985.
Bachelor of Arts in History, University of Montana, Missoula, Montana, 1978.

PROFESSIONAL CERTIFICATION

Washington Basic Teaching Certificate, Grades 5-12—Social Studies, Language Arts.
Alaska Basic Teaching Certificate, Grades 5-12—Social Studies, Language Arts.

PROFESSIONAL HONORS

Outstanding Service Award, Bethel School, Bethel, Alaska, 1991.
Participant, National Endowment for the Humanities Summer Seminar for Secondary School Teachers, University of Chicago, Chicago, Illinois, 1989.
Participant, Summer Program in Leadership and Administration, Montana, 1980.

REFERENCES AVAILABLE UPON REQUEST

ANTHONY WYATT
3892 MAIN STREET #485
ALBANY, NY 12207
518•555•3398

OBJECTIVE: A challenging position as media planner/market researcher for an advertising corporation or department

WORK EXPERIENCE

Host, writer and **producer** of the nationally syndicated Fishing Line radio program. Duties include all phases of research; establishment of contacts; in-person, mail, and phone interviews. Responsible for all aspects of creation and electronic production of 1/4-inch master audio tapes. In 1989, the program was syndicated to 100 radio stations. 1985-present.

Public relations, marketing coordinator for Fishing Line Communications Network. Responsible for affiliate radio station PR service via phone, mail, or personal appearance. Assist in locating suitable corporate sponsors and convincing them of the merit of advertising via the network. 1981-1985.

Reporter, news anchor, talk show host, disc jockey, commercial production, announcer, editor for WCLA, WRDD-FM, WSLY AM-FM-TV, WSKY-FM, WPKR-AM, and WPBB-FM, Albany Public Radio. 1972-1980.

Instructor, Broadcast Arts, Ronald Pembroke School of Broadcast, Pilsberg University. Presented formal classroom lectures, chalktalks, equipment demonstrations, and guidance. Subjects included: copywriting, newswriting, interviewing, editing, and production. 1972-1980.

PUBLICATIONS

Salmon Fishing the Atlantic Salmon, published 1988.
"Backpacking for Adirondack Trout," *Fishing Adventures Magazine,* Spring 1988.
"Brook Trout Fishing in Upstate New York," *Fishing Adventures Magazine,* Fall 1987.
Write monthly column for *Outside Air,* circulation 8,000, New York State.

EDUCATION

Coursework toward Master of Arts in Communications (10 credits), State College of New York. 1991-1992.
Bachelor of Arts, Broadcast Journalism, Pilsberg University, Albany, New York. 1970.

CONFIDENTIAL RESUME AVAILABLE UPON REQUEST

WILLIAM T. PETERS
83920 WESTERN AVENUE
SAN ANTONIO, TX 78284
(512) 555-2983

OBJECTIVE:

A POSITION AS PUBLIC SCHOOL ADMINISTRATIVE ASSISTANT

WORK
EXPERIENCE:

Office Manager, Bryant & Bryant Tax Consulting, San Antonio, 85-present
Organize office and procedures; organize and maintain client files; prepare bank statements; receive and record payments; prepare bills; perform word processing, typing, and chart preparation using WordPerfect, Microsoft Word, Lotus, PageMaker, and Works on the IBM.

Accounting Clerk, B & S Accounting, San Antonio, 80-85
Performed word processing; maintained accounts payable and accounts receivable, general ledger, billing, and payroll; answered phones; greeted clients; processed mail.

Clerical Assistant, Paul Ginnis, CPA, San Antonio, 78-80
Updated tax libraries; typed various tax forms; processed tax returns; filed; answered phones.

Secretary/Receptionist, Century 21 Real Estate, San Antonio, 71-78
Personal assistant to office president; typed legal documents; greeted clients; answered phones; maintained accounts payable, accounts receivable, and billing; screened prospective renters; prepared work orders and invoices; wrote and updated rental listings; placed ads; checked renters out of units.

RELEVANT
EXPERIENCE:

Volunteer, San Antonio School District, 89-present
Assisted in elementary, junior, and senior high offices; provided computer entry, filing, and student file processing support.

Member, PTA Committee, San Antonio, 85-present

EDUCATION:

A.A., Liberal Studies and Business, 71
Temple Junior College, Temple, TX

REFERENCES: FURNISHED ON REQUEST

M E L I S S A　　P A R K E R

254 Bingham Drive • Durham, North Carolina 27701 • 919-555-9338

OBJECTIVE

A teaching position in the field of graphic arts

EDUCATION & TRAINING

Teacher's Certification, Art
University of North Carolina at Greensboro, 1992

Tutor Training, Carolina Literacy League
Durham Public Library, Durham, NC, 1985

Certificate, Applied Graphic Design
Carolina Junior College (2-year program), 1975

B.A., Art History
University of Georgia, Athens, 1973

RELATED WORK HISTORY

Graphic Artist / Support Staff
Atlantic College of Design, Durham, NC, 1985-1993
Responsible for production of all material needed for academic functions of college. Assisted instructors in development of materials and curricula for core courses in the graphic arts. Served as art and computer consultant. Produced teaching materials for instructors. Developed reference library of slides, books, journals, and articles. Taught computer courses on Macintosh.

Graphic Artist / Typesetter
TIP Printing, Durham, NC, 1980-1985
Managed all in-house typesetting, design, and production for business printer, increasing shop's production capabilities extensively. Proofread copy, produced mechanicals and photostats. Designed projects for clients. Wrote copy for projects. Assisted in bookkeeping and billing. Consulted with and assisted clients in design, copywriting, and Macintosh use.

Production Artist / Office Manager
Popper Typesetting, Durham, NC, 1975-1980
Responsible for all aspects of production work in typesetting shop. Proofread copy, produced mechanicals and photostats. Assisted in design and copywriting.

REFERENCES ON REQUEST

Margaret Samuelson
3131 Mountain Drive
Longmont, CO 80501
(303) 555-2435

Objective
Senior editorial role with a major trade book publisher.

Skill Highlights
Management and organizational experience.
Editing in a variety of subject areas, including literary and scientific/technical materials.
Excellent communication skills and extensive writing experience.

Education
B.A. (Honors) in English, 1972, University of Colorado, Boulder, CO

Editorial and Publishing Experience
1984-present—Managing Editor, University of Colorado Press, Boulder, CO
Responsible for the day-to-day management of this scholarly press. Responsibilities include
    *Solicitation and evaluation of book manuscripts
    *Development of financial projections and plans, including print run numbers and prices
    *Coordination of production schedules, print specification plans, editing, design
    *Development and implementation of marketing and promotion plans

1983-1984—Editorial Assistant, Environmental Studies Department Publications, UC
Duties included editing, styling, and proofreading papers on environmental studies related topics; writing bibliographic annotations; and compiling lists of new publications.

1983-1990—Literature Editor, Aspen Books, Denver, CO
As a volunteer editor, assisted in evaluating fiction and poetry and making publication decisions. Assisted with copyediting, layout, proofing.

1979-1982—Assistant Editor, Boulder Weekly, Boulder, CO
Evaluated material submitted and made publication decisions, wrote articles and reviews, coordinated the calendar section, assisted with layout and proofing.

1975-1979—Editor, Plainfield House Textbook Publishers, Denver, CO
Editorial duties included soliciting and evaluating manuscripts; preparing copy for press; proofreading; corresponding with authors. Attended educational and trade conferences for the company.

1972-1975—Editor, Manhattan University Press, Manhattan, KS
Responsible for an extensive list of English as a Foreign Language books. Duties included soliciting and evaluating manuscripts; drawing up contracts with authors and overseas distributors; working with authors to ensure relevance to curriculum requirements; editing and re-writing manuscripts; coordinating the work of designers, artists, and printers; photograph research and commissioning artwork; planning and writing publicity materials; and supervising the production of taped language materials.

References on Request

ROSE K. REID

4893 PEYTON DRIVE
PITTSBURGH, PA 15205
412-555-2938

OBJECTIVE: A position as Coach for a Division I or II women's collegiate gymnastics team

COACHING/GYMNASTICS EXPERIENCE AND HONORS
- Coach and manager of Pawtucket High School gymnastics team, 1980-82
- Assistant coach, Hanson Gymnastics School, Portsmouth, NH, 1976-80; Gymnastics coach, Woodman Camp, Woodman, PA, and UNH Sports Camp, Durham, NH, 1978-80.
- Eighteen years of gymnastics training and participation in team, high school, and college gymnastics.
- Member, Pennsylvania Gymnastic Judges Association, Gymnastics Judge at state high school and club meets, 1980-present.
- Volunteer Gymnastics Coach, Pittsburgh YWCA, 1983-present.
- As Captain of University of New Hampshire team, 1979-80, provided leadership for 14 team members, acted as a liaison between athletics and administration, served as representative of athletics at University and community functions.
- Two-time honorable mention to Atlantic 10 Academic All-Conference Team, 1979-80.
- Set two UNH gymnastics records while qualifying as an individual for the NCAA Regional Championship in 1979.

WORK HISTORY
Technical Sales Officer, BIOTECH Inc., Pittsburgh, PA, 1984-present
Coordinate sales effort in Mideast region for this environmental consulting firm. Responsible for locating new customers and for supervising current accounts. Act as liaison between company and customer. Assist customers in completing sample collection. Coordinate shipment, analysis, and reporting.

Laboratory Technician, BIOTECH Inc., Pittsburgh, PA, 1982-84
Completed standard tests on site samples. Coordinated job routing through laboratory.

Pharmacy Technician Aide, VA Medical Center, Springfield, MA, 1980-82
Compiled weekly drug accountability figures. Acted as pharmacy link to computerization of inpatient accounts. Filled prescriptions.

Gymnastics Coach, Pawtucket High School, Springfield, MA, 1980-82
Instructed, devised progressional programs, and choreographed routines. Organized team trips and season schedule. Coached and supervised team of 25 high school girls.

Assistant Gymnastics Coach, Hanson Gymnastics School, Portsmouth, NH, 1976-80

Gymnastics Coach, Woodman Camp, Woodman, PA, and UNH Sports Camp, Durham, NH, 1978-80.

EDUCATION
International Seminar, Israel, Peace & Understanding Through Sport, January 1982
B.A., Biology, 1980, University of New Hampshire, Durham, NH
GPA: 3.53, Phi Kappa Phi Honor Society, Dean's List, 6 semesters, Extensive coursework in Sports Medicine and Training

REFERENCES ON REQUEST

PARKER M^CMILLAN 389 Broker Hill Road Bloomfield, MI 48103 313 555-0900	PROFESSIONAL RESUME
OBJECTIVE	A POSITION IN HUMAN RESOURCES MANAGEMENT
PROFESSIONAL EXPERIENCE	**Educational Consultant and Trainer**, Bloomfield School District, Bloomfield, MI 1987-present Develop and run training groups for professional growth, cooperative learning, curriculum integration, and peer coaching. Extensive work between administration and staff and among staff members to promote better working relationships. **School Library Media Specialist**, Fort School, Bloomfield, MI 1973-1987 Designed and supervised a library media center of 38,000 print and non-print items for resource-based curriculum. Supervised three para-professionals. Acted as liaison and resource specialist for staff and administration. Served as Staff Development Center liaison, Chair of Social Studies Curriculum Committee, team teacher with classroom teachers, grant writer, cooperative learning mentor, and Chair Media Council. **Director**, Pillham Regional Junior High School Library and District Media Processing Center, Bloomfield, MI 1969-1973 **Head Librarian**, Baker High School, Boston, MA 1967-1969
EDUCATION	**Ed.D. Division of Instructional Leadership**, School of Education, University of Michigan, Flint, 1987. **M.L.S. Library Science**, Graduate School of Simmons College, Boston, MA, 1967. **B.A. English Literature**, Boston College, Chestnut Hill, MA, 1965.
REFERENCES	Provided on request.

Adam T. Carlisle

389 LaSalle Boulevard
Little Rock, Arkansas 72201
Voice: 501-555-3823
Fax: 501-555-9987

Objective
A position in the promotion department of a book publishing house, particularly for a publisher of children's books.

Qualification Highlights
- Managed an independent children's bookstore
- Buyer in the trade department of a University bookstore
- Coordinated a reading series in an independent bookstore
- Produced a bookstore newsletter using PageMaker on a Macintosh

Work History
- Manager, Donkey and Giraffe Books, Little Rock, Arkansas. *1987-present.*
  Supervise and manage all operational procedures of bookstore.
  Co-buyer for new titles.
  Hire and supervise two staff clerks.
  Develop merchandising and displays.
  Coordinate schedules.
  Develop promotional events.

- Events Coordinator, Dusty Sage Bookstore, Stillwater, Oklahoma. *1983-1986.*
  Developed and organized a reading series that continued to grow after the first year, increasing sales 20 percent and providing a unique event for the community.
  Developed publicity and promotional material for the series, and developed special offers to increase sales, including production of a newsletter.
  Handled all merchandising and displays for the store.

- Assistant Buyer, Trade Department, Oklahoma State University Bookstore, Stillwater, Oklahoma. *1980-1983.*
  Responsible for buying all non-text book titles in the store.
  Met with publishers' sales representatives about new forthcoming lists.
  Analyzed customer interests, developed section backlists.
  Analyzed sales figures, determined and adjusted order quantities.

Education
Coursework in Children's Literature and Graphic Arts, Oklahoma State University, 1986.
B.A., English Literature, Oklahoma State University, Stillwater, Oklahoma, 1980.

References
Available upon request

Joseph Bigelow
12582 Highway 92
Billings, Montana 59124
(406) 555-2947

Experienced supervisor seeking new challenges in project management with a public or private organization in Billings.

What I can offer	What I've accomplished	How your firm can benefit
12 years supervisory experience	developed staff of corporation so that promotion comes from within after the first 2 years	reduce employee turnover save in training costs
effective business management skills	planned growth through budget control and reduced costs by 23 percent in the first year	save money that can be reinvested in the company to increase growth opportunities
	expanded company growth by 30 percent in the first year	increase production efficiency without increasing staff
people-oriented management style	reduced employee turnover to less than 2 percent per year	a stable, happy employee group providing increased production
strong sales leadership	received Peak Award and Embassy Award for sales efforts	a proven track record of achievement
solid marketing skills	redesigned product that produced $570,000 in new territory in the first year	increased income and sales opportunities for existing company products
familiarity with distribution channels for several industries	established distributor network that increased company market share by 37 percent in first year	increased sales and reduced distribution costs
effective planning skills	developed business plans that netted measurable results within a given time frame	increased sales revenue and reduced production costs

Employment History

Gates Rubber Company, Denver, Colorado, Regional Sales and Distribution Manager, 1985 to 1993
   Division Sales Manager, Denver, 1982 to 1985
   Plant Production Supervisor, Denver, 1978 to 1982
   Plant Sales Manager, Denver, 1975 to 1978
   Plant Warehouse Manager, Denver, 1973 to 1975
   Warehouseman, Denver, 1970 to 1973

Education

B.S., Business Administration, University of Denver, Colorado, 1975

references provided on request

Lydia Diaz
2983 Pomona Road
South Valley, NM 87105
505-555-2224

Objective

A management position in sales/shipping with a retail mail order sales company.

Work Experience

Office Manager, *Boys and Girls Club of South Valley, 1979 - present*
 Coordinate activities and procedures between department chairs.
 Act as intermediary in dealing with the public and with wholesalers.
 Organize the office and its procedures, program supplies, and inventory.
 Update and maintain membership lists and coordinate direct mailings.
 Maintain computer databases and files.
 Produce and distribute the club newsletter.
 Coordinate community events and club calendar, edit and proofread.
 Coordinate production of booklets, fliers, and tickets for athletic events.

Research/Clerical Assistant, *Office of International Research and Development, State of New Mexico, 1971 - 1979*
 Researched and compiled data on various subjects.
 Input data and maintained database on IBM computer with dBase III+ software.
 Provided general clerical work—typing, filing, answering phones.
 Gained computer experience with WordPerfect, MS Word, Lotus, and Harvard
  Graphics.

Sales Associate/Receiving Clerk, *Lamont's, Albuquerque, NM, 1967 - 1970*
 Held three-quarter-time job while completing bachelor's degree.
 Assisted customers with purchases.
 Operated cash register and handled cash, check, and credit card transactions.
 Opened and closed register and maintained responsibility for accuracy of receipts.
 Prepared displays for windows and within store.
 Received merchandise into the store and assisted with stocking.

Education

B.A. Business and History, University of New Mexico, Albuquerque, 1970.

References upon request

Chapter Six

SAMPLE COVER LETTERS

P.O. Box 1254
Sioux Falls, S.D. 57103
March 21, 1993

Public Relations Manager
Bryson Department Store
Fourth & Main Streets
Sioux Falls, S.D. 57114

To the Public Relations Manager:

I would like to submit the enclosed resume for your consideration in hiring the next Customer Service Manager at Bryson. My experience in public relations, marketing, and sales combine to offer you more than the required qualifications listed in your position announcement.

As the Assistant Director for Public Relations at Morris Brothers, I worked closely with consumers who had purchased or were interested in learning more about our products. In cases of complaints from consumers, I quickly and efficiently determined the problem and achieved a solution that met both the consumers' needs and the corporation's goals.

In sales and marketing, I have worked on a variety of market research projects and coordinated targeted promotional campaigns. I have also held supervisory positions in both sales and public relations.

After you have reviewed the enclosed resume, I hope you will call me at 555-3828 so that we can discuss both your expectations and the qualities I can bring to the position. I look forward to an informative discussion.

Sincerely yours,

Judd Riley, Jr.

15 March 1993

Human Resources Director
Search Committee: Senior Technical Editor
Merrick Engineering, Inc.
P.O. Box 223
Rutland, Vermont 05702

To the members of the Search Committee:

Enclosed please find my application for the technical writer/editor position currently available at Merrick's Rutland office.

From the Environmental Computing Center to the new University Theatre and an endowed professorship in integrated circuit design, I have written, edited, and coordinated more than 150 grant proposals for many of the University of Vermont's most significant projects. As Proposal Writer for the University's Foundation and Development office, I work closely with vice presidents, deans, directors, and faculty to present their projects to both lay and technical audiences. I directly supervise two staff members and a student assistant, and coordinate the efforts of others involved in the grant-writing and fund-raising process within the University.

My graduate work in English and undergraduate studies in pre-medicine at Stanford have prepared me to write with ease on a variety of topics. I've edited complicated research presentations for many of the University's premier scientists while also working with leading scholars in the humanities to prepare fund-raising documents for various cultural programs.

My experience as a free-lance writer, graphic designer, and photographer further qualify me for this position. Two of my recent publications present biographies and in-depth research abstracts on scientists featured in *Nobel Prize Winners: Physiology and Medicine.*

Your prospectus requested salary requirements. As my primary interest in the position is in the challenges it offers to put my skills to good use for a company that has a strong international reputation for excellence, I would be satisfied should the proposed remuneration meet my current gross annual income of $45,000, which includes salary and benefits.

I will be out of town until the 19th, after which I will be happy to meet with you. I would value the opportunity to join the strong and growing team at Merrick, and I appreciate your review of my application.

Sincerely,

Amanda Wentworth
26 West Parade Drive
Rutland, Vermont 05702
802-555-9847

J. WILLIAM CLARK
4437 WHITE OAKS DRIVE
URBANA, IL 61801
(217) 555-2847 (VOICE)
(217) 555-3345 (FAX)

Mr. Arthur Davidson
Director
Davidson & Beckfield Associates
Suite 110, Ridley Tower
Chicago, Illinois 60621

Dear Mr. Davidson:

I was delighted to talk with you yesterday about your interest in hiring a public affairs director, and I want to restate my interest in learning more about the position.

So that you might learn more about my background, I have enclosed a summary resume for your review. If you prefer, I can forward my complete dossier, along with recommendations from professional associates.

What captures my interest about this position is the possibility for effecting change on a significant scale. My previous experiences have offered tremendous opportunity for influencing the country's growth in positive ways, but within fairly limited spheres—education and domestic economics, primarily. I have continued my involvement with social policy and public administration while lecturing at the University, and I am more convinced than ever that there is a great need for an organization like yours to turn its attention to unifying these issues in a direct and meaningful way. That is a challenge I would find immensely rewarding, both personally and professionally.

Our mutual friend, Helen Ashwood, told me I could find no more professional and respected an organization with which to align my efforts. After the discussion you and I shared this morning, I clearly agree with her astute assessment.

Therefore, I look forward to talking with you again soon.

Best regards,

Bill Clark

February 21, 1993

Frank Martin
Jones Martin Construction Co.
3356 Highway 36
Pocatello, Idaho 83251

Dear Mr. Martin:

I am writing to apply for the Foreman's position listed at the Human Services Division Office. Enclosed is a resume listing my previous work experience.

For the past 15 years I worked as the Supervisor at Twin Peaks Plywood Mill, where I was responsible for 24 workers on a shift. I also scheduled workers for two other shifts. The closure of the mill has prompted my return to construction work, which I did successfully as a union carpenter for nearly 10 years in the 1970s.

I believe my construction background together with my supervisory experience provide the qualifications you are looking for in a construction foreman. I have worked on both single- and multiple-family housing as well as several-story office buildings and am familiar with building codes in Idaho as a result of building my own home in 1986.

I would like to call and make an appointment to talk with you, or you can reach me at 555-6682. Thank you for considering my application.

Sincerely,

Joseph W. Caldwell
346 Buena Vista
Pocatello, Idaho 83251
(208) 555-6682

21 March 1993

Corrine Bracken
Executive Director
Design Engineering
20 West Tenth
Dallas, Texas 76443

Dear Ms. Bracken:

In reply to your advertisement in the Wall St. Journal March 15, I am enclosing a professional resume and letters of recommendation for the position of Vice President of Sales and Marketing.

I believe the executive management positions I've held with DaMark-Dolin America since 1982 have given me the experience and capabilities you are looking for in a top marketing executive. As DaMark-Dolin has recently been acquired by InnaVail Corp., I have chosen to seek new opportunities and challenges within the corporate management sphere.

I have taken the liberty of calling to arrange for an appointment to speak with you further in order that I might learn more about your expectations and how I might make a significant contribution toward Design Engineering's future progress and growth. I look forward to meeting with you on April 5.

Best regards,

Angelita Bergman

Darius G.W. Harms
3485 Plainfield Road
Lincoln, Nebraska 68573
402-555-9287

March 1, 1993

Jonathan Parker
Engineering Division Director
State of Nebraska
P.O. Box 5678
Lincoln, Nebraska 68570

Dear Mr. Parker:

Please accept this letter and the enclosed resume in application for the Engineering Supervisor position announced February 25.

I believe my extensive background in structural and mechanical engineering meets or exceeds the qualifications you are looking for. I have served both as a senior engineer and as an engineering supervisor with responsibility for 120 workers.

For my part, I would like to put my expertise and experience to work for the benefit of public works projects, where safety and quality form the guiding values, as stated in your position description. Too often in the corporate world, the demand for higher profit margins takes precedence over innovative developments and worker safety. My experience in this field, however, has given me the ability to achieve desired results in the most efficient manner possible, thus cutting costs and increasing productivity.

Please review the enclosed resume and call me at the number above. I would very much like to talk with you about the position and what my experience can bring to your department.

Yours truly,

Darius Harms

Margaret Samuelson
3131 Mountain Drive
Longmont, CO 80501
(303) 555-2435

April 1, 1993

Susan Franklin
Personnel Director
Specialist Books
P.O. Box 2362
Denver, CO 80235

Dear Ms. Franklin:

Please accept the enclosed resume and letters of recommendation in application for the Senior Editor position with the Science & Technical Division of Specialist Books. I am responding to the position announcement listed in the March 26 edition of Publishers Weekly.

Currently I am Managing Editor of the University of Colorado Press, with full responsibility for acquisitions, development, design, and production. The position has been an extremely rewarding one, but statewide budget cuts within higher education have resulted in the indefinite closure of the press.

Therefore, I would like to put my energy and extensive publishing background to work for Specialist Books in your Science and Technical Division. Approximately 65 percent of the titles I published with the UC Press were of a scientific or technical nature, and I gained additional editorial experience in the field as Editorial Assistant for the Environmental Studies Department of the University.

I would be happy to forward copies of relevant publications—both initial manuscripts and final publications—as examples of my editorial work. I would also appreciate an opportunity to discuss the position with you personally. I can be reached at the above number after hours and on weekends, and at 555-0429, ext. 23, during the week.

I look forward to receiving your call and thank you in advance for your consideration.

Yours sincerely,

Margaret Samuelson

GLORIA SANTOS   *2534 COLLINS AVENUE • MIAMI, FLORIDA 33239 • 315 555-8906 •*

March 25, 1993

Pat Newton
Personnel Director
Lane Michaels Associates
345 Main Street
Miami, Florida 33219

Dear Pat Newton:

In response to the March 18 advertisement for a Financial Resources Associate in the Miami Herald, I am submitting the enclosed resume and salary requirements for your consideration.

For the past 13 years I have worked as an accountant and office manager for a variety of organizations. My interest in the financial resource management of these organizations led me to return to graduate school at the Florida International University for a certificate in financial management, which qualifies me as a financial resources counselor and securities adviser.

My coursework involved extensive study of economic theory, policy, and practice, as well as the specific methodologies of financial analysis and resource management. My previous experience as an accountant served me well in pursuing study in these areas, and I believe it has allowed me to bring a unique perspective to the analysis and management of finance.

I would like to meet with you to discuss the position and your requirements in more detail, as well as present further support for my specific qualifications for the position. I am available at the number above any day after 2:00 p.m. and on weekends. I look forward to talking with you, and thank you for your consideration.

Sincerely,

Gloria Santos

1233 Mission Street
San Pablo, California 98329
January 20, 1993

Personnel Director
Bakersfield & Associates
Box 123
San Pablo, California 98332

Dear Director:

Please accept the enclosed resume in application for the position of Associate Sales
Director, which was advertised in the San Francisco Chronicle last week.

After an interesting and rewarding career as an engineer, I returned to graduate
school in 1991 to pursue a growing interest in business, specifically in marketing and
sales. Early in my career, I gained some valuable experience as the Engineering Sales
Specialist for Shell Oil Company. In this position, I worked with manufacturers and
small business owners to coordinate efforts for fuel efficiency and cost savings. The
marketing and sales program that resulted was the most successful in the company's
history.

During my graduate program at Oregon State University, I worked closely with
several faculty members in consultation with a major technology manufacturer in the
area to recast the company's image and stimulate sales in a slogging economy. The
strategic planning sessions with corporate executives provided a tremendous on-the-
job training opportunity for me as a graduate student, and the project achieved the
desired results.

My inquiries have revealed that your firm has a strong reputation for excellence and
innovation that makes me eager to bring my skills in strategic planning and market
analysis to work for Bakersfield & Associates.

I would appreciate an opportunity to discuss the position with you further. Please call
me at 212/555-0812, where messages may be left if I am personally unavailable.

Thank you for your consideration.

Sincerely,

Donna Everson

Joan P. Yolen

**20876 Hopewell Avenue
Aurora, IL 60507
708 555-3833**

February 19, 1993

Andrew Martin
Executive Director
Sheraton Hotel
600 Shoreline Drive
Chicago, IL 60615

Dear Mr. Martin:

I am enclosing my resume and three letters of reference in reply to the position announcement for Personnel Director at the Chicago Sheraton Hotel.

I believe you will find that my experience has provided me with the qualifications you are looking for in your top personnel officer. I have held several managerial positions with responsibility for personnel issues, including handling union negotiations and safety regulations. I am also well-versed in payroll accounting and the required quarterly tax reports.

As you will note from the enclosed letter from my current employer, David Harris of Jordan Distributing, the downsizing of the corporate management structure has left no clear path for advancement within the organization. While I have enjoyed my tenure with Jordan, I am interested in taking on new challenges, particularly in the area of personnel management.

Once you have reviewed the enclosed material, I would appreciate an opportunity to talk with you further. I can be reached at 708-555-7465 days, and the above number evenings and weekends. I look forward to talking with you.

Thank you for your consideration.

Sincerely,

Joan P. Yolen

143 NW 19th
Everett, WA 98215

March 2, 1993

Mr. Jack Dunn
Superintendent
Everett School District
P.O. Box 16394
Everett, WA 98235

Dear Supt. Dunn:

John Nokes in your department recommended that I write to you to express my interest in the Associate Principal's position currently being advertised for the Everett Junior High School. Enclosed you will find a summary resume.

After several years with increasingly responsible positions in the Bethel School District in Alaska, I have returned to my home town with the desire to continue my career in education administration. I believe my educational background and classroom and special programs experience give me the qualities needed to be a successful associate principal.

Most recently I was involved in a special project to develop an incentive program for boosting school attendance. The program brought together a broad base of community support and provided an opportunity for children to learn more about their own cultural backgrounds as well as that of others in the community. It was a tremendous success. At a time when educational support from taxpayers is faltering, it is imperative to develop timely, location-specific programs to get people re-involved in our schools. I look forward to the challenge of stimulating my home town to greater public support for the school programs.

I will call your office early next week to schedule an appointment to speak with you further about the position and my qualifications. If you would like to reach me before then, I am available at 206-555-9283. I look forward to meeting with you soon.

Sincerely,

Andrew Vizenor

ROBERT L. WILSON JR.

1854 South Franklin Avenue, Chicago, IL 60647 • (312) 555-8376

January 19, 1993

Jane K. Shapiro
Director of Development
Art Institute of Chicago
16 Bayshore Drive
Chicago, Illinois 60602

Dear Ms. Shapiro:

I am very interested in applying for the position of Communications Specialist in the Development Department at the Art Institute. Please find enclosed a brief resume and some samples of publications for which I have served as editor and designer.

As a member of the cultural "scene" in the Chicago area for the past 10 years, I have lately felt a need to get more directly involved in helping the arts continue to thrive, not just survive. Toward this end, I have recently sold the magazine I owned and operated, with the intent to take an active role in arts support and advocacy. I believe my dedication as well as my skills in the communications media will serve the position profitably.

After you've had an opportunity to review the enclosed material, I would like to meet with you personally. I can be reached at the above number, or I will call you by the end of next week to schedule an appointment. I am eager to talk with you further about the position and how I envision my contribution to the Institute. Thank you for your consideration.

Sincerely,

Robert L. Wilson Jr.

MAIA JOINER • 24 Wellington Place • Tallahassee, Florida 32311 • 904-555-6787

January 16, 1993

Susan Winslow, Director
Public & Corporate Relations Department
Hammond Powell Hyde and Carter
24 W. Broadway, Suite 1215
Tallahassee, Florida 32301

Dear Ms. Winslow:

Please accept this letter and the enclosed resume in application for
the position of Public Relations Associate for broadcast production
currently open at Hammond Powell Hyde and Carter.

For the past 25 years, I have worked in the broadcast media industry
and gained a wealth of knowledge of media affairs, public interests,
and corporate communications. I believe the perspective I bring from
my background on the "other side of the fence" will serve me well in
your department.

My technical background in electronics and video technology have also
proven invaluable when producing video programs and advertisements.
With a thorough understanding of <u>how</u> such a program is made I can use
the medium to its best advantage.

I would like to show you some footage from several of the projects I
have worked on, both recently as production engineer for the Channel 5
News at Noon and from my tenure as Public Relations Associate for
WJKE-FM Radio.

Thank you for your consideration. I look forward to hearing from you.

Sincerely yours,

Maia Joiner

Arthur Lewis
789 Hansborough Street
Boston, Massachusetts 02169
617 555-8962

February 21, 1993

Dr. Frank Parminter
Executive Director
Department of Health and Human Services
452 Center Street
Suite 3305
Boston, MA 02135

Dear Dr. Parminter:

Thank you for sending the information I requested concerning the Public Information Officer position currently available with your department. I would like to apply for the position, and am enclosing my resume and the requested letters of recommendation and salary requirements.

I can bring to this position some unique skills gained through several years as a language arts instructor in the high school system. Teaching writing and communications skills is perhaps the best possible way to expand and refine one's own skills. I have also developed strong public presentation skills as well as knowledge of production processes for printed publications.

I would like to have an opportunity to talk with you further about the position and the specific strengths I can bring to your department. I will call your office early next week to schedule an appointment at your convenience.

I look forward to meeting you and learning more about the program areas the department covers. Thank you for your kind attention.

Sincerely,

Arthur Lewis

Juanita Rodriguez-Sutton
330 Hollywood Boulevard
Los Angeles, California 90063
(213) 555-2475 days
(213) 555-0248 eves

March 26, 1993

Jefferson Grant
Director
Hollywood Ad-Man
443 La Ciernica Boulevard
Hollywood, California 90028

Dear Jeff:

I enjoyed talking with you Thursday about the A.D. position with Hollywood Ad-Man. After our discussion, I came away convinced that I'm the woman for the job. Once you've reviewed the enclosed resume and agency list, I believe you'll agree.

You mentioned that one area not currently covered by staff members' experience is research and market analysis — that you've had to contract this work out or rely on hunches and suppositions. I can bring extensive experience in both areas to take some of the guesswork out of strategic planning and target advertising.

I've also had significant experience with broadcast media, both radio and television. Given the trend in advertising today toward a reliance on cable television outlets, additional experience in this area could be a strong plus for your company.

I will call you next week to talk more about the job and what I can bring to the position. Again, I enjoyed our conversation and look forward to meeting with you soon.

Best regards,

Juanita Rodriguez-Sutton

Tucker Wendell
P.O. Box 12597
Cincinnati, Ohio 45204
513/555-9041

March 18, 1993

Glynnis Martin
House of Imoja
1257 S. Patterson
Cincinnati, Ohio 45212

Dear Ms. Martin:

I am writing in application for the youth training coordinator's position announced in Sunday's issue of the Cincinnati Gazette. Enclosed please find a resume and statement of philosophy, as requested in the position description.

Your program works with disadvantaged youths of various ethnic backgrounds, and I believe I am highly qualified for the position—not because I have all kinds of degrees in psychology or sociology, because I don't. My qualifications lie in my having been right where these kids are when I was their age, faced with seemingly insurmountable odds against any kind of success. I learned the hard way to set my sights on achievable goals, then go after them one step at a time, always believing in my ability to succeed. Perhaps more than anything these young people need role models who have shared their feelings of disenfranchisement but who have carved their own new directions and new meanings of success.

As employment and training manager for Food-Pac Corporation, I have worked extensively with young people—many of them high-school dropouts—who saw a job on the food processing line as the dead end of their dreams. By developing a program of cross-training—which allows workers to train in areas of special interest in addition to the line work—I have been able to help many youths see a new pathway and go on to achieve a different dream.

I found this the most rewarding aspect of my job, and as a result have become involved in a variety of youth-oriented programs. I would now like to devote my attention full-time to helping stem the crisis among our youth, especially those living in urban areas like Cincinnati. I hope to talk with you soon to discuss your program and how I can contribute to its success.

Please call me after 5 p.m. or on weekends at the number above, or I can be reached during the day at 555-2785, ext. 213. Thank you for your consideration. I look forward to hearing from you.

Sincerely,

Tucker Wendell

KARL LI

290 SUMMIT DRIVE
PORTLAND, OR 97208
503 555-0709

April 16, 1993

Sibyl Jameson
Vice President, Marketing & Sales
Simmons & Wooster, Ltd.
21 Grand Street
Portland, OR 97210

Dear Ms. Jameson:

I was delighted to talk with you yesterday about the sales manager's position currently open at Simmons & Wooster. As you requested, I am forwarding a summary resume outlining my previous experience in the world of non-profit corporation development. I have also . enclosed some sample publications produced under my direction at both the Willamette Valley Health Care Foundation in Portland and the Children's Foundation in Chicago.

In many ways, the worlds of fund-raising and sales are very closely related. In both, one asks a potential patron to part with hard-earned income in exchange for some kind of return. With fund-raising, my job was to persuade patrons of the value of such intangible returns as a lasting kindness or a tax deduction come April 15th. Marketing also plays an extremely important role in fund-raising activities—presenting a strong "corporate image," the need to keep the corporation in the public eye, "selling" a potential donor on something as elusive as a concept.

In my familiarity with the quality of the products and services provided by Simmons & Wooster, I can say with certainty that developing and directing sales campaigns will be both stimulating and rewarding. I am looking forward to our April 26 meeting so that we can further discuss your expectations for this position and how my background can bring some fresh insights to the role of sales manager.

With best regards,

Karl Li

FAITH NUYGEN ❖ 775 Tilbury Road ❖ Fresno, California 93723 ❖ (209) 555-7623

February 6, 1993

Ms. Ellen Carlson
Senior Director
California Department of Economic Development
One Government Plaza
Sacramento, California 95813

Dear Ms. Carlson:

Thank you for the information you sent in regard to the Project Manager's position with the CDED. I would like to submit the enclosed application and resume for your further consideration.

I have worked with the Consortium of California Counties since 1981, and I believe I have found my niche in the area of project management. I have handled a wide range of projects with increasing levels of managerial responsibility. Most recently, I directed the planning, coordination, and management of a major statewide conference on job training, which involved the participation of several international specialists. I was given less than two months to manage the entire project, and yet the result received appreciative reviews from all participants.

After twelve very rewarding years with the Consortium, however, I am aware that I have reached the extent of opportunities for advancement within the organization. Therefore, I am looking forward to new challenges, and would very much like to join the impressive program at CDED.

I can be reached at (209) 555-2984 during the days, and at the number above for messages as well as evenings and weekends. I look forward to hearing from you and discussing how I might contribute to your program.

Sincerely,

Faith Nuygen

BRIAN WEBLEY •• 345 Coral View, Apt. 9B •• Coral Gables, Florida 33128 •• 305•555•7823

February 27, 1993

Personnel Director
Patterson Printing
Box 1263
Miami, Florida 33551

Dear Sir or Madam:

I am writing to apply for the Production Manager position advertised in Sunday's edition of the Miami News. Enclosed is my resume and statement of salary requirements.

In my 23 years with the printing industry, I have worked primarily as a mechanical or operational engineer concerned with the technical end of the printing machinery. More recently, I have developed an interest in and discovered a facility for managing the front end of the business—production and press preparation. As Manager of Graphic Arts Engineering for the D.E.C. Printing Group, I took on increasing responsibility for the management and facilitation of the production processes in addition to the engineering concerns of the equipment. During my tenure in this position, I implemented programs that increased efficiency by approximately 35 percent and thus significantly increased the company's profit margins.

By concentrating my energies more fully on production management, I believe I can achieve significant gains for Patterson Printing as well. Once you have reviewed the enclosed material, I would like to talk with you further about your organization and how I might become a part of your team.

I look forward to hearing from you.

Sincerely,

Brian Webley

JONATHAN B. OWENS
2245 RIVER ROAD
NEWPORT, OR 97366
503 555-2435

31 March 1993

J. Paul Murray
Executive Director
Human Services Consortium
State Office Complex, Suite 743 B
Salem, Oregon 97310

Dear Mr. Murray:

After 20 years of active duty in the U.S. Coast Guard, I am ready to move inland and take on new challenges in a civilian career in program development and implementation. I would like to bring my experience in training and curriculum development to work for you in the position of Management Specialist III. In response to the position announcement in the Oregonian March 26, I am submitting the enclosed application for your review.

My most recent responsibilities with the Coast Guard involved the development, design, and implementation of a curriculum for training Coast Guard personnel in emergency response and medical training. I was responsible for selecting and evaluating a staff of 35 for the Central Training Center. In addition, I established a new computer system to improve communications, which utilized electronic mail and enabled instant communications with Coast Guard facilities around the world.

I would like to speak with you personally about the position and my unique qualifications. Please call me at the number above, and I will be delighted to travel to Salem to meet with you at your convenience.

Thank you for your consideration. I look forward to talking with you.

Sincerely,

Jonathan B. Owens

VGM CAREER BOOKS

CAREER DIRECTORIES
Careers Encyclopedia
Dictionary of Occupational Titles
Occupational Outlook Handbook

CAREERS FOR
Animal Lovers
Bookworms
Caring People
Computer Buffs
Crafty People
Culture Lovers
Environmental Types
Fashion Plates
Film Buffs
Foreign Language Aficionados
Good Samaritans
Gourmets
Health Nuts
History Buffs
Kids at Heart
Nature Lovers
Night Owls
Number Crunchers
Plant Lovers
Shutterbugs
Sports Nuts
Travel Buffs
Writers

CAREERS IN
Accounting; Advertising; Business;
Child Care; Communications;
Computers; Education;
Engineering;
the Environment; Finance;
Government; Health Care; High
Tech; International Business;
Journalism; Law; Marketing;
Medicine; Science; Social &
Rehabilitation Services

CAREER PLANNING
Beating Job Burnout
Beginning Entrepreneur
Career Planning & Development for
    College Students &
    Recent Graduates
Career Change
Careers Checklists
College and Career Success for
    Students with Learning Disabilities
Complete Guide to Career Etiquette
Cover Letters They Don't Forget
Dr. Job's Complete Career Guide
Executive Job Search Strategies

Guide to Basic Cover Letter
    Writing
Guide to Basic Résumé Writing
Guide to Internet Job Searching
Guide to Temporary Employment
Job Interviewing for College
    Students
Joyce Lain Kennedy's Career Book
Out of Uniform
Slam Dunk Résumés
The Parent's Crash Course in
    Career Planning: Helping Your
    College Student Succeed

CAREER PORTRAITS
Animals; Cars; Computers;
Electronics; Fashion;
Firefighting; Music; Nursing;
Sports; Teaching; Travel; Writing

GREAT JOBS FOR
Business Majors
Communications Majors
Engineering Majors
English Majors
Foreign Language Majors
History Majors
Psychology Majors

HOW TO
Apply to American Colleges and
    Universities
Approach an Advertising Agency and
    Walk Away with the Job You Want
Be a Super Sitter
Bounce Back Quickly After
    Losing Your Job
Change Your Career
Choose the Right Career
Cómo escribir un currículum vitae
    en inglés que tenga éxito
Find Your New Career Upon
    Retirement
Get & Keep Your First Job
Get Hired Today
Get into the Right Business School
Get into the Right Law School
Get into the Right Medical School
Get People to Do Things Your Way
Have a Winning Job Interview
Hit the Ground Running in Your
    New Job
Hold It All Together When You've
    Lost Your Job
Improve Your Study Skills
Jumpstart a Stalled Career

Land a Better Job
Launch Your Career in TV News
Make the Right Career Moves
Market Your College Degree
Move from College into a
    Secure Job
Negotiate the Raise You Deserve
Prepare Your Curriculum Vitae
Prepare for College
Run Your Own Home Business
Succeed in Advertising When all
    You Have Is Talent
Succeed in College
Succeed in High School
Take Charge of Your Child's Early
    Education
Write a Winning Résumé
Write Successful Cover Letters
Write Term Papers & Reports
Write Your College Application Essay

MADE EASY
Cover Letters
Getting a Raise
Job Hunting
Job Interviews
Résumés

OPPORTUNITIES IN
This extensive series provides
detailed information on nearly 150
individual career fields.

RÉSUMÉS FOR
Advertising Careers
Architecture and Related Careers
Banking and Financial Careers
Business Management Careers
College Students &
    Recent Graduates
Communications Careers
Education Careers
Engineering Careers
Environmental Careers
Ex-Military Personnel
50+ Job Hunters
Government Careers
Health and Medical Careers
High School Graduates
High Tech Careers
Law Careers
Midcareer Job Changes
Re-Entering the Job Market
Sales and Marketing Careers
Scientific and Technical Careers
Social Service Careers
The First-Time Job Hunter

VGM Career Horizons
a division of *NTC Publishing Group*
4255 West Touhy Avenue
Lincolnwood, Illinois 60646–1975